The Lost is Found

A "Lost Boy's" Story of Faith,
Hope, Charity, and Love

JACOB THON GUOT

lynne, Thank you for your great
support.
July 17, 2018
Blessings,
Rev. Jacob Guot

All Scripture quotations, unless otherwise indicated, are from The King James Version. The KJV is public domain in the United States.

Scriptures marked NIV are taken from the NEW INTERNATIONAL VERSION (NIV):Scripture taken from THE HOLY BIBLE, NEW INTERNATIONAL VERSION ®. Copyright©1973, 1978, 1984, 2011 by Biblica, Inc.™. Used by permission of Zondervan

Scriptures marked NLT are taken from the HOLY BIBLE, NEW LIVING TRANSLATION(NLT): Scriptures taken from the HOLY BIBLE, NEW LIVING TRANSLATION, Copyright©1996, 2004, 2007 by Tyndale House Foundation. Used by permission of Tyndale House Publishers, Inc., Carol Stream, Illinois60188. All rights reserved. Used by permission.

ISBN: 978-1-945975-25-7

Published by EA Books Publishing a division of
Living Parables of Central Florida, Inc. a 501c3
EABooksPublishing.com

DEDICATION

This book is dedicated to the "Lost Boys" of Sudan
and to the many friends who have encouraged me to write it.
I also dedicate it to the great country of America,
which has provided me with God's protection, peace,
citizenship, education,
and the resources with which to write.

CONTENTS

ACKNOWLEDGMENTS

I write this book to share the experiences and struggles I survived as a "Lost Boy" of Sudan. The book is written in remembrance of my family, relatives, and friends whom I lost on the run from Sudan, from Ethiopia, and even while here in America.

I have been through darkness, but the darkness is the birth of a new dawn, and it should be welcomed rather than dreaded. A new dawn could restore hope to the South Sudanese people who have lost three generations of progress as a result of the long civil war.

This book would have not been possible without the help of my wife, Rebecca Athieng Deng, who endured a grueling immigration process in Africa with our infant son, Biar Guot, to join me in the United States. After she came, she spent many hours with our son and our other children, Angeth Guot and Ayiei Guot, while I was working, attending school, and writing this book. Rebecca and I celebrated my graduation from Lancaster Bible College and Asbury Theological Seminary with great joy. We saw how God had been with us in the hardships we have endured, the people we have met, and the long journey we have had. All of these things have contributed to our lives and have gone into the preparation of this manuscript. We are eager to see what God has ahead for us.

I would like to thank all the citizens of America who contributed their energy and resources to help solve the complex problems of Sudan and South Sudan. I want to thank presidents George W. Bush and Barack Obama, as well as their administrations, which pressured the Sudanese to work together for peace. Many churches in the United States have also been involved in the efforts to bring peace to the Sudanese and have helped the "Lost Boys" who came to the U.S. Oprah Winfrey must also be thanked for supporting American intervention in the conflict between Northern Sudan, Darfur, and South Sudan, and for her efforts in building a school for girls in South Africa.

So many people in Texas and Pennsylvania are worthy of my thanks. Many people in Houston gave Rebecca great encouragement, especially Erin and Jason Knesek, Summer and

Tim Simmons, and Jamie and Chris Daighdrill. Thank you to Patrick and Stephanie Jue, who gave tremendous help to my ministry and educated my brothers in Africa. They said, "Without education there is no progress at all."

Jerry and Nancy Dumas have my undying gratitude for supporting me in so many ways. They helped me come to Asbury Theological Seminary and have supported me financially. I am also grateful to many members of the First United Methodist Church of Lancaster, Pennsylvania. The former pastor, Kent Kroehler, and his wife, Joy, also supported my going to Asbury Theological Seminary. They believed in me. Kent always said, "God is bigger than us." He is absolutely right about that.

I would like to thank Pastor Terry and his wife, Vickie, and the members of First United Methodist Church in Odessa, Texas for helping with an apartment. Thanks to many members of St. Luke's United Methodist Church in Midland Texas. I am grateful for my pastor, and now Superintendent, Richard Edwards for his friendship, hospitality, kindness, willingness to help, and support of my ministry. I would like to thank Lancaster General Hospital in Lancaster, Pennsylvania for canceling 100% of our expenses for my wife's treatment. Without their wonderful generosity we would be overcome with debt. I would also like to acknowledge Lancaster Gastrological services for forgiving 95% of our debts to them. I praise God that we have been able to pay this debt in full.

I appreciate our former Bishop of the Diocese of Bor, the Rt. Rev. Nathaniel Garang Anyieth, for his humility and for the service he provided without pay during the war, and for ministering to many Sudanese. My thanks to uncle Rekeboam Akechditt Kuai Biar, the first generation of our family.

I am grateful for those who are now or have been in places of power in South Sudan.

Our president, Salva Kiir Mayardit, needs our prayers and support. I am thankful for the late Dr. John Garang de Mabior, who was the founder of the Sudan People's Liberation Movement/Army, which fought the Sudanese government and forged the Comprehensive Peace Agreement, which led to the formation of the new nation of South Sudan. Thanks also to Michael Makuei Lueth, a lawyer and key person in the South Sudanese peace negotiations. I am also grateful for Governor Kuol

Manyang Juuk, one of the visionary leaders who fought hard to protect our people.

Many teachers and caretakers have been helping us in the refugee camp and deserve my gratitude. Among them are Maker Thiong Mel, Joseph Maker Kur, Rev. Thomas Angau Kur, William Bul Lual, Deng Dau Malek, and others who have invested in us. I am also very thankful to all our elders who have been with us many years and have shared their counsel and wisdom with us: people like ReecAthooc Reec Kuol, uncle Ayom Anuur, late uncle Apiou Anyar, uncle Akuot-Maketh, Akech Luk, and others.

The east African countries of Ethiopia, Kenya, Uganda, Rwanda, and Tanzania allowed us to be refugees in their countries. I am especially grateful to the people of Uganda and to their President, Yoweri Museveni, for the protection they have given the South Sudanese refugees within their country and for helping them keep their respect and dignity.

My personal thanks goes to the people at Asbury Theological Seminary, especially my mentor and editor Dr. Robert Danielson, and also to Dr. Steve Ybarrola, Sheila Lovell, Skye West, and Gabrellen Pfarr.

Introduction

The Red Sea, Nubia, and the Land of Cush are terms with which most biblical students are familiar. If you locate these areas on a map, you have located Sudan. The northern desert lands of Sudan reach up to Egypt, and the Red Sea and Ethiopia form its eastern borders. The area of Southern Sudan becomes flooded swamplands during the rainy season and supplies water for many rivers, which feed northward into the White Nile, the Sobat, and the Blue Nile, eventually joining together as they flow through the desert lands of northern Sudan and into the great Nile of Egypt. A series of highlands are scattered throughout the swamplands of southern Sudan. These lands are where the black tribes of South Sudan have settled. Their lives are centered around the raising of cattle and subsistence farming on the community lands. In biblical times, many trade routes wound through these lands. Camel trains of merchants and caravans of pilgrims traveled from Egypt through the Nubian Mountains and the the bush in southern Sudan, trading their wares and looking for places to settle.

During the day of Pentecost in Jerusalem, after the crucifixion of Jesus, over three thousand people became converts. Many of them became missionaries who joined these caravans and spread Christianity throughout East Africa. Long before Christianity moved westward to Rome, it was thriving in the churches of Sudan and Ethiopia. For six hundred years, Christianity grew along the eastern trade routes, reaching as far as China and the South Sea Islands.

Sudan was the largest country in Africa before it was essentially divided in two. It contains a vast range of contrasts, as seen through the equatorial rainforests and swamps in the South, through the mountains of Nuba, Jebel Marra, and the Red Sea

1

area, and through the Sahara Desert in the North. During the rainy season, the roads and tracks become thick streams of mud. The heat can become intense during the day, yet it can be cold at night, especially in the desert areas, where it can even reach the freezing point. The South is covered by savannah, elephant grass, swamps, and forests, which support elephants, buffaloes, lions, cheetahs, leopards, giraffes, zebra, hippos, antelope, chimpanzees, baboons, and crocodiles, as well as snakes, scorpions, and tsetse flies.

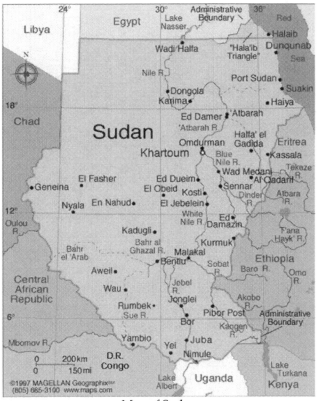

Map of Sudan

Sudan has the potential to be a wealthy country. The Red Sea hills have substantial mineral deposits, and there are oil reserves in the southwest and northwest. West Africa's largest river, the Nile, flows through Sudan, which gives it immense agricultural and pastoral potential. However, the Sudanese are some of the poorest people on the planet. International human rights and relief agencies rate Sudan as among the five countries in the world with the worst score on the "human suffering index." In terms of the availability of clean drinking water, daily calorie intakes, education, political freedom, civil rights, and life expectancy, Sudan's rates are the world's highest in suffering and the lowest in freedom. What was once called the "breadbasket of North Africa" has become the site of the worst man-made famine in the world. About two million people have died since 1983 as a result of either the war or the famine. Five million more people have lost their homes and are internal refugees.

These conditions were the result of the conflicts between the Arab Muslims of the North and the Southern people. Mohammad's cultural background was greatly influenced by Christianity, and he and his followers accepted Jesus as a great prophet. When Christians rejected Mohammad's ways, he became their adversary and began to form his oppositional forces. Since then, these lands have been a battleground between Christianity and Islam. In the 13th century, internal Christian squabbling and a massive Arab immigration led to the rise of Islam in northern Sudan. By the beginning of the 19th century the Ottoman Turkish influence overran the whole country.

At the beginning of the 19th century, the Ottoman ruler of Egypt, Mohammed Ali, launched a series of attacks on Sudan. He was a ruthless and power-hungry army officer who had gained control of Egypt with the help of the Mamluks, a mercenary military class who were originally Turkish slaves. Later when the Mamluk leaders posed a threat to Mohammed's power, he eliminated them all by massacring them at a banquet he had called in their honor. Mohammed's son, 25-year-old Ismail, set out with 10,000 men to raid Sudan. Ismail's troops were promised 50 cents for every human ear they brought back. Three thousand ears and 30,000 slaves were sent back to Cairo, but only about half of the slaves survived the journey. The Sudanese then counterattacked, and Ismail died a fiery death in his tent. Mohammed retaliated with more invasions. By 1823, over 50,000 Sudanese had been killed, and Sudan was firmly under Egyptian control.

After the building of the Suez Canal, and when the Egyptian government became bankrupt, Britain became the dominant power in both Egypt and Sudan. In 1873, the Christian General Charles Gordon was appointed governor, and his campaign to stamp out the Islamic slave trade created a crisis in the Muslim community. Open rebellion erupted.

Mohammed Ahmad, a local Muslim leader declared himself Mahdi, which is a military messiah selected by Allah to lead a Jihad, or holy war. He began the Mahdiyya Movement, which has continued to influence Islamic politics in Sudan to this day. The Mahdi rampaged throughout Sudan and destroyed the forces of General Gordon. They were on the way to overcoming all of Sudan when they were finally destroyed in 1898. After that, Sudan had almost 60 years of relative peace, and slavery was effectively suppressed.

In the 1940s, England recognized the devastation that the Muslims were imposing on the Black tribes of southern Sudan through the slave trade and the exploitation of southern Sudan's rich wildlife, supplying ivory and exotic animal skins for export. The English stepped in and brought a semblance of peace to the area. The English Anglicized many of the southern tribal peoples, and the Dinka tribes of the Bor area of southern Sudan were among them.

When Sudan declared its independence in 1956, a civil war erupted between the Arab north and the black south. In 1972, the Addis Ababa Agreement temporarily ended the war by granting the south autonomy and religious freedom. However, this peace was shattered in 1982 when the Islamic dictator, Col. Nimeiri declared Sharia Law (Islamic law) over all of Sudan. When our tribes resisted the Sharia Law imposed by the Arab Islamic government of Sudan in 1982, the Muslims began horrendous persecution of the Black Christian tribes of southern Sudan. John Garang, a Sudanese graduate of Iowa State University and a member of the Dinka tribe, headed the Sudanese People's Liberation Army (SPLA). In two years he had 25,000 armed soldiers under his command. However, the SPLA became weakened by tribal infighting, but John Garang kept fighting the Sudanese Government with a vision to bring about New Sudan. He created a political movement called the Sudan People's Liberation Movement (SPLM) to widen his influence among many people both in the north and the south. When Nimeiri left power,

Sadiq became the Muslim head of the northern leadership, and he responded to the SPLM by arming Baggara Arab militias in western Sudan to raid and plunder the southern part of the country. They attacked and burned villages, stole livestock, poisoned wells, and killed men, women, and children fleeing to safety. This is what led to the "Lost Boys'" predicament.

On July 30, 2005, Garang died in a mysterious helicopter crash. Salva Kiir was made the leader of the SPLM and acting president of Southern Sudan. In 2010, Kiir focused on independence for South Sudan and on July 9, 2011, the Republic of South Sudan became a new nation in the world, and Salva Kiir Mayardit its first president.

Between the war and the famine, two million people have lost their lives since 1983, and five million more people have lost their homes and are internal refugees. In addition to all of this, bandits continue their plague of robbing, torture, and murder in western Sudan.

The new government of South Sudan is struggling with many issues, just as any new government would. They have a big job to do. They seem to be making progress in areas such as making good diplomatic connections with important countries and continuing to defend their borders in the North. South Sudanese outside the country have the role to walk alongside and support those in the new country as they hammer out the details of the new government.

SOUTHERN SUDAN MAP BY COUNTY/STATE

Map of South Sudan

1
My Dinka Childhood

Most people in America have heard of the "Lost Boys" of Sudan, of which I am one. We are called "Lost Boys" because beginning on May 16, 1983 and continuing through the following 22 years, the Muslims and the Christians have been fighting a devastating war. As a result, many of us lost our parents, our homes, our friends, and our communities. However, we did not lose our faith, our minds, our hearts, our dignity, or our ability to persevere.

My family and I are members of the Dinka tribes who live in the southern area of Sudan. The Dinka are the largest single national grouping of people in South Sudan, numbering about two-and-a-half to three million people and constituting more than 25 aggregates of different Dinka sections called *Wut*, a word which means "cattle herder's hut." In earlier times, the Dinka did not live in villages, but traveled in family groups. Their homesteads might be in clusters of one or two families up to a hundred families. As the Dinka established their administrative centers, permanent small towns grew up, composed of many extended families. The Dinka culture retains the traditional pastoral life.

The customs of the tribal people are built around the preservation of family. They have earned a reputation of being honest, trustworthy, reliable, and peaceful people. They were Anglicized in the early 1900s, but they continued to accept and practice polygamy since it was their historical custom and was practiced in the Old Testament. It is the fathers' responsibility to provide for their families, especially in the training of their boys to become responsible men. Fathers also make sure that their wives train their daughters to be kind and capable women. A father also has the responsibility to provide for all of his wives in an equitable way that will not cause stress in the family. For the children, the process of getting to know all of their relatives is considered a privilege and a duty. They try to visit all of their relatives' homes and are expected to show respect and love for each relative at all times. No written records of the elders or the members of the community exist, because the children learn the history of the family and community as they progress in life. In turn, the relatives have the duty to help with the discipline and nurture of all the children.

My true birthday is unknown, but my recorded birthday is January 1, 1980. I was born in Jalle Payam, a community in the southern part of what was then known as the country of Sudan. My family named me Thon Guot Ayiei; Guot being my father's name and Ayiei being my grandfather's name. But when I became a Christian, I adopted the name of Jacob. My father was the sixth child of his parents and was a farmer. He raised livestock – cattle, goats, and sheep. He knew the strengths and weaknesses of each of his animals and knew how to breed them so that the offspring would carry the best characteristics of both parents.

In my culture, the number of cattle, sheep, and goats a man owns demonstrates the measure of his wealth. Cows and bulls are by far the most valuable assets. Cows are important because they provide milk and cheese, which are very marketable and are important for a healthy diet. Both animals are also important because our village life is centered around tribal celebrations and family gatherings that call for the slaughtering of cows and bulls for wonderful feasts which accompany every important celebration. Above all, every young man needs access to good cows to provide a dowry for him to choose a good wife. A man who has a large quantity of fine cows and bulls, like my father did, has the opportunity to marry the finest of the young women of the tribes.

I was the first son, which meant that at the early age of five I helped my father care for his livestock. I drove the livestock to the public grazing lands early in the morning and made sure they returned safely in the evening. At this young age, I was also in charge of the goats. The land surrounding our villages was a mix of bush, grasslands, swamps, and farmlands. There were no fences, so those of us who cared for the livestock had to watch our animals so they did not get lost or harmed. For me, keeping track of the animals was difficult, especially when they disappeared into the tall grass. Big cows did not present such a problem to herders, but goats and sheep could easily disappear. The tall grass could also hide a lion, a hyena, or a thief who wanted to steal one of the animals, so I had to be constantly on my guard. I also had to make sure the animals did not wander onto another farmer's field where they might destroy or eat another man's crops. If this happened, the farmer might kill or harm the animal, and he would also report it to my father, who would be very angry that I had not been responsible enough to control the livestock. When this happened, my father would have to compensate the farmer for any losses.

Our dog, Marol, was my constant companion, and I depended upon him. He knew my friends, and if a stranger were in the area, he would growl and chase them away. Sometimes our animals would get mixed with other people's animals and I would have to separate them. This was a huge responsibility for a boy to handle. As the oldest son, I not only had a responsibility to my father, but also had to set an example to the younger members of my family.

I generally left home at 8:00 a.m. and returned around 6:00 p.m. My very active little mind would often think about what to do if something unexpected occurred – if someone decided to kill me, steal an animal, or if a lion attacked. Should I stay and be killed, or should I run away and leave the animals? Once, while I was looking after goats and calves with Marol, I heard a lion roar. Marol began to whine, and then he ran away. What was I to do? Without my dog, I could not keep track of the animals. If I ran after Marol, I would have to leave the animals, and if they destroyed someone's field or crops it could lead to hard feelings towards my family, retaliation, or even war if the victim had a bad attitude! I was not sure of the lion's location in the high grass. If I saw him and ran, then he would attack my animals. If I did not run, then he might attack and kill me, and the animals would still be lost! I prayed to God, but how would I know what God wanted me to do? I wanted to do a good job because I knew that, as the oldest son in the family, I would be taking over from my father when he got old. Any irresponsible action could put my future in jeopardy. All of these questions went through my head in what must have been a split second. I decided to run after Marol. We came back to tend to the animals, and the lion never showed up. Those days of herding were sometimes scary, but mostly they brought happy memories for me.

I remember the lush pasturelands where Marol and I would bring my father's little flock of sheep and goats to graze. Today, those pasturelands are overgrown with bush and dense growth where wild animals hide. The lowlands are flooded and marshy, and alligators roam through them. During my boyhood, our villages were clusters of neat, well-built homes with shelters and well-built fences for the animals. Clean paths and roads connected each village together. Gracious shade trees grew all around. There were chickens, cows, goats, dogs, and children everywhere. Every yard had a table or two where the women prepared food or dried clothes, and there were chairs and hammocks nearby where friends could fellowship and rest. Now, many of these villages are sad-looking places. The houses are in disrepair. Many of the roads and paths are overgrown and littered with trash. The water running through the ditches along the roads is dirty, yet this is where many people get the water for their homes.

My mother used to clean and dress me well when I left the house with my dog, but now the children wear torn and worn-out clothing, or no clothing at all. In my boyhood, when I left my home to take my father's livestock to pasture, I had a purpose and a destination to look forward to. Now, so many children are standing around with nothing to do and with sad faces. During my free time, I would play with the other boys, watch the older boys playing games in the fields, or sit patiently, listening to the older folks tell stories and share the news of the villages. Now, much of this way of life has been disrupted. So many of the young people have left for the military or have been killed, and the old folks are often left alone to fend for themselves. Medical issues abound in every family, but there are no doctors to help them and no medicines available for them. When I last visited, I walked many miles to get medicine for some in my village, but it was never enough.

In 1905, British Anglicans sent missionaries to my people in the southern part of Sudan to establish churches and bring us the

Bible translated into Dinka, our native language. I was born into the church, and my family life pretty much centered around the church. It is the custom in our tribe for the parents to take their children to church so that they learn about Christ and what is expected in the way of biblical behavior. However, this made us enemies of the Muslims who ruled the Sudan from the desert lands in the north.

Some of my happiest childhood memories are of the church in my village. I loved the singing and hearing the preacher tell us about the ways of Jesus. I loved when we gathered to share food and news. Tribal dancing was often a part of our church celebrations, and I loved watching and participating in it. In church, we became one community as we prayed together, shared together, and cared for one another. As a boy, I was not aware of the human side of church, where some were snubbed and others bragged about their accomplishments, showed off their wealth, or gossiped. To me, church was where everyone was good and life was happy. I now recognize that no church is perfect, but it is still the place where God's ways are taught and where people are nurtured to make progress as they work towards God's ideals.

THE LOST IS FOUND

2
Ritual Scarification

From ancient times people have decorated their bodies by marking through tattooing or scarification. Tattooing usually involved shallow cutting or pricking with ash or some kind of pigment rubbed into it, forming permanent marks on the skin. Scarification has been used mostly among dark-skinned, equatorial peoples where there is so much melanin in the skin that a tattoo would hardly be noticed. Scarification is a more severe form of marking that involves deeper cuts than tattooing. It is done with a very sharp knife and results in distinctive scars. The skin is skillfully cut, and sometimes raised with fishhooks or some similar tool, so that ashes or dirt can be rubbed into the wound, causing a more noticeable scar. The scarification process in most of these cultures is a male ritual, marking the transformation from infancy to manhood. For many centuries, African people have used scarification as an expression of cultural identity, community status, and connection to our ancestors or gods. In almost all hunting and gathering cultures, the shedding of blood summons the gods and the good and evil spirits.

The pain and blood in the scarification process play a large part in demonstrating a person's fitness, endurance, and bravery. This is especially the case in puberty rites, since children must prove they are ready to face the realities and responsibilities of adulthood, in particular, the prospect of injury or death in battle for men and the trauma of childbirth for women.

Over the centuries, my Dinka cultures have established a very complex and highly effective hierarchy of power and rights. These tend to run along influential family lines and there can be severe consequences for those who do not respect them. This type of tribal cultural hierarchy has fostered the practices of markings and scarifications that are found in the traditional Dinka cultures, for they represent various badges of honor dignifying one's rank in the tribe. Dinka boys receive scars to mark their transition to manhood when they take on the responsibilities of a man. A man without scarification may be judged as being either a coward or as coming from an unworthy family. In either case, he does not have the backing or the respect of the tribal powers. Such a person would not be trusted with his own cows, nor would the girls view him as a desirable mate. He also would be at a great disadvantage among those who conduct business in the villages. People would not trust him, so he would not be able to conduct any business transactions.

The scarification ceremony usually takes place for a boy between the ages of ten to sixteen. A boy dare not cry or show fear during the scarification ceremony because it would be a sign of weakness, which would bring dishonor to his family. Courage, aggressiveness, and violence are some of the most important characteristics of a Dinka man and they are key elements in an initiation.

I received my scars at a very young age. The night before the ceremony, as the ritual requires, we boys gathered together to spend the night singing the songs of our clans. This time of singing is a way of strengthening the boys collectively and psychologically preparing them for the ceremony. Our heads had already been shaved in preparation for the initiation ritual itself. At dawn, the boys are collected by their parents (particularly their fathers), and taken to the ceremonial place. After receiving a blessing, the boys take their places in a long row, sitting cross-legged with the sunrise at their backs. As the initiator comes to each boy, the boy calls out the names of his ancestors. The boys have been trained from birth to respect and fear these ancestors who have the spiritual power to harm those who displease them or disrespect them.

It takes a skilled person to do the scarification. The initiator clasps the crown of the boy's head firmly and pushes it against the blade of his very sharp knife, making the proper number of three to six cuts to match that particular clan's pattern. The cuts are sometimes very deep, and ashes or dirt are sometimes applied to make the scarring more pronounced. The boys must look straight ahead and continue reciting the names of their ancestors. When all of the initiates have been ritually scarred, their fathers wipe the blood from their sons' faces and then wrap a broad leaf around their foreheads.

I remember sitting in the line of boys and young men of my tribe, waiting for my scarification. I was proud of myself for being brave and not crying. I was filled with exaltation as I imagined the great warrior I would be. I delighted in my father's pride in my power over evil as he tenderly cared for my wound. I was in no way prepared to acknowledge my need for God in my life!

My Dinka tribal markings are the six lines cut into my forehead, going from the hairline towards the front, almost meeting just above the middle of the forehead. When I arrived in America during my teen years, I found myself experiencing a totally different reaction to my scarification. Americans looked at my scars with great pity. To them, such wounds represented some kind of accident or tragedy and they could not understand that the marks were a badge of honor, especially in the middle of my forehead! When I explained that they were tribal markings, I remember how humiliated I was to be judged as more "primitive" and less "advanced" than they were. It took me a long time to adjust to their judgment. I had to learn to forgive their ignorance.

When the Dinka become believers, we are set free from the tribal rituals and the powers of their evil spirits through Jesus Christ, who cleanses us from all our sins and makes us holy in God's sight. Now, we have fellowship with God rather than with our ancestral spirits and customs. Now, rather than priding ourselves on our many scars and looking down upon those who are weak, we rejoice in our freedom in Jesus and fellowship with our brothers and sisters in Christ, even the weak ones. Now, we worship and praise God together and support one another as we grow in our walk with Jesus. This is why I would not support the practice of scarification in my African church, nor will I perform the ceremony for my sons.

Scarification does have its negative aspects. Although they are the largest single national grouping of people in South Sudan, the Dinka constitute more than twenty-five aggregates of different sections. Competition is fierce, not only for the scarce resources of the land, but for the rights and power over these resources. Inevitably, there are problems when several tribes lay claim to the same paths or to the same resources. This leads to harassment between tribes. In those cases our scarification would work against us, as we would not be able to hide our identity. It has also worked against us when opposition tribes wanted to do us great harm. There was no way for us to blend in with the rest of the population.

More seriously, our scarification marked us for death by the Muslims. As we were being persecuted and driven out of our cities during the Muslim takeover of our country, we had to hide in the bush and send various tribal members into the towns and cities to beg for food and water. We had to be very watchful for any Muslim soldiers who might spot our scarification and recognize us as their enemies.

3
I Become A "Lost Boy"

Boys and girls of the Dinka tribes grow up living the greater part of their lives in the company of their peers. From a young age, they eat together, learn their tribal dances, and assume their roles as they fellowship together. This means they usually form closer relationships with their peers than they do with their families.

As children, we had very little knowledge of the deep conflicts that had been boiling for decades between the ruling Muslims in the north and the Christians in the south. We were not aware that the Muslim government of Sudan had used the *Foreign Missionary Society Act of 1962* to classify churches as foreign rather than domestic entities. This allowed them to forbid the construction of churches without strict government permits and to burn many existing churches. Some pastors and elders were even crucified. We were not aware that the Muslim government of Sudan was planning another deadly offensive against our area's Christian community, whose numbers had grown due to our peaceful and well-managed lives.

In the spring of 1987, at seven years of age, I was guarding my family's herds in the village of Bor-Jalle. I slept with the cattle, while my father, mother, and siblings slept at home. Suddenly, in the middle of the night, we were awakened by the deafening sound of gunfire. We had never made a plan of escape for such an attack, so my family scattered, everyone running for their lives. In those horrifying moments I did not realize that I would never see my father again, and it would not be until May 9, 2006 that I would see my mother after that awful night. That night, I became a "Lost Boy."

The terrible sounds of weapons' fire and exploding bombs filled the night air. The Muslim government of the North attacked us with bombs from the air and shot the people as they scattered. I was bewildered, not knowing where to go or what to do. Suddenly I was swept up in a huge crowd of people fleeing for their lives into the wilderness. I was surrounded by men, women, and children from many villages as we moved en masse for miles and miles in the hot, humid bush. People had been forced to run with whatever they had on. Those who had worn no shoes soon had blistered, bloody feet. Those of us who had been in the fields had a bottle of water and provisions for the day, but most did not. That first night was the most horrible night I had ever experienced. I felt so alone without my parents, siblings, or any relatives at all.

Although this attack had taken the younger people by surprise, many of the older men and women had seen the signs and suspected that a raid might happen. The leaders among us had already been investigating options. They had heard that neighboring Ethiopia might give us some protection.

The Dinka custom was to arrange the members into large tribal communities called *Payams* to ensure that all of the people were protected and supported. Our leaders told us that we had no hope of trying to return to our villages, so we should immediately start walking to Ethiopia. We formed ourselves according to our Payams and walked in single file and stayed close to one another. I did find some cousins in my Payam, and I stayed closest to them. The Payam not only provided us with care and fellowship, but also gave us protection from other Sudanese tribes who were not friendly to ours, and from Sudanese criminals who were wandering throughout the land robbing others.

I do not know how far we walked that night, but I remember being exhausted when morning came. We did not dare travel during the day because it would be too dangerous. Not only might the soldiers see us but, without food and water, it was unwise to stay in the blazing sun. We hid during the day, and marched single file at night. We passed through miles of bush, which harbored dangerous animals like snakes and lions. We journeyed over barren wilderness while avoiding elephants and hyenas. We trudged through swamps filled with snakes and crocodiles and traversed through hostile scrublands. The leaders cared for the thousands of us during our long march, and all of us were called upon to make life-and-death decisions. We endured thirst, hunger, and danger of death. I thought I was going to die several times, as did so many of my friends. God protected me on this nightmare journey.

These routine attacks on the Christian villages of southern Sudan left many boys as orphans. Because most boys had been away from their villages tending cattle, sheep and goats, we were able to flee and hide with others in the dense African bush. Some of the unaccompanied male minors were conscripted by the Southern rebel forces and used as soldiers in the rebel army. Others were handed over to the government by their own families, who were assured that they would be fed, cared for, and sent to school. However, most of them were either killed or forced to fight in the Muslim army.

THE LOST IS FOUND

4
Escape To Ethiopia

Ethiopia was more than a thousand miles away. We walked, and walked, and walked through the hot, humid bush, getting what food and water we could from begging. Sometimes we got so desperately thirsty that we used our urine to wet our mouths or to wet the dirt in an attempt to eat it. When we fled, we had only the shirts on our backs and the pants or shorts we wore on our ever-moving legs. How we wished for a change of clothes, a blanket to keep us warm at night, or a pair of shoes to protect our feet. After several weeks of traveling, I remember going to sleep at night and waking up with no expectation of anything good or positive in my future. I cried often when I was off by myself, so no one would notice.

Approximately 1,000 miles of desert and tribal lands existed between Sudan and Ethiopia. It was a very dangerous area to traverse in any circumstance, but especially dangerous on foot, with few or no supplies, while being hunted. We began to pass through the tribal lands of the Murle people. They are wanderers without close ties to other communities. They live in some of the most hostile desert and scrublands, which cannot support large family groups. Over the centuries, they have made a living by robbing those who pass through and by kidnapping children to sell as workers and to people who do not have children of their own. For the Murle, this way of life has become a very lucrative business. At every rest stop, they would bring their cows to us and offer them as trade for some boys and girls. I could not understand why they thought the children were for sale, but our leaders understood the situation. Our group was too large for them to kidnap anyone. Knowing that we would be starved for food, they tried these different tactics. It took many weeks to cross their territories, so our leaders soon made them understand that our children were not for sale. Still, we had to be very watchful because they were always looking for an opportunity to kidnap any of the children who might be on the fringe of the traveling community.

We continued our journey towards Ethiopia, walking mostly during the night, so as not to be detected. During the hot, sweltering days, we would try to construct some kind of shelter to hide from the sun and get some rest. The sound of thousands of moving feet during the night and the strong scent of unwashed human beings attracted the attention of the surrounding wild animals. We could see them slinking alongside us, waiting for a vulnerable person to become separated from the crowd so they could be seized. One night a lion interrupted our line, and we scattered in two directions in much confusion. But we regrouped ourselves quickly and continued in spite of our fear. Many times when we settled down for the day, some of the animals would boldly move into camp. We were terrified by the constant sounds of various animals surrounding us. When a herd was near, we became very quiet and cautious because a stampede of these large animals could kill many people. We had very few guns and clubs to protect us. Everyone had to be vigilant both day and night.

The rainfall in the highest mountains of Ethiopia had been heavy that year. Our journey took us through rivers and swamps where recent rainwater had saturated the areas to the flood stage. The brush and grasslands hid cobras and pythons, but the enormous reptiles became increasingly dangerous when we crossed through the swamps. Since pythons and crocodiles wait for their prey in swamp waters and on banks of rivers, we had to be very, very watchful. We waded fearfully through the waist-high water with our hands up, hoping no pythons or crocodiles were waiting to make a meal of us! The rivers were an even larger problem since most of us did not know how to swim, and at flood stage, the rivers were all running very fast. When we came to a river we needed to cross, some found piles of dead wood and debris to hang onto. Some waded out as far as they could and then struggled in the water until they drowned or found the river bottom. Others found ropes and swam with one end to the other side so that people could hang onto them while crossing. At one river, someone found five old canoes from the Anuak tribe. The tribe graciously gave them to us, and some of our people piled into them and started across. However, the inexperience of the people coupled with the strong current in the middle of the river caused them to overturn and most of them drowned. This brought about yet another threat. Their dead bodies attracted crocodiles which would then head for any boat they saw. The rivers terrified us, but we had no alternative to crossing them.

We reached Ethiopia after many months of grueling travel across the desert, through the bush, over rivers, and through swamps. When we arrived, we were not sure what to expect. We were informed that the Ethiopian government had set up a camp for us in the area of Panyundo, which is in the Oromo tribal territory on the border between western Ethiopia and Sudan. When we arrived at the camp, we discovered that it already contained over a thousand refugees from Sudan. After we settled, we regrouped to assess our situation. We discovered that our group had lost over a thousand people, mostly boys and girls. This was a time of deep sadness. I remember being surrounded by the sounds of weeping and mourning. None of us will forget that terrible journey in the year of 1987. But we had to face the fact that the rest of us were alive, and we had to continue.

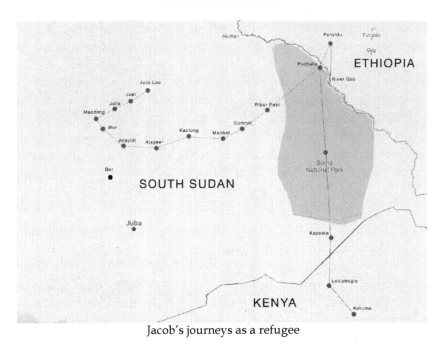

Jacob's journeys as a refugee

5

Panyundo Refugee Camp

In Panyundo we again arranged ourselves according to our Payams. This allowed every Payam to have a designated shelter or tree area where they could keep track of their children and tribal members. Then, in small groups, we quickly set about to cut and gather wood and grass for tiny shelters. Our shelter fit five boys; I was the youngest. However, three of our number soon died of illnesses, and the two of us remaining were left feeling very sad but very fortunate at the same time. By now, all of our food was gone. Most of us still had only the same clothes we fled with, which had not been washed for weeks. They were full of lice, which made our skin irritable and itchy. The foul water, lack of food, and unsanitary conditions caused many to suffer from fever, diarrhea, and typhoid. Thousands died from malnutrition and disease, and those of us who were left were not strong enough to bury them. Sadly, hyenas often dug up and ate those who were buried. The wild animals fed on so much human flesh that they became emboldened and would even attack the living.

The United Nations High Commissioner for Refugees (UNHCR) came to visit our refugee camp and could not believe what he saw. In less than a week, a tractor-trailer of food was sent. Then, both the UNHCR and the Red Cross Agency arrived from Addis Ababa, which is the Ethiopian capital in the far north. The Red Cross did a head count, and we were told about sixteen thousand of us had survived and were living in the camp. We were given food, water, clothing, a pair of shoes, and a blanket. These were very precious gifts to us.

The Red Cross brought medical supplies, set up dispensary camps, makeshift clinics, and a sort of hospital, but they were overwhelmed and understaffed. They used anyone who spoke a little Arabic or English and could read or write even a little bit to help them. No pharmacist was available, and the only person who could write a prescription was the tired, overworked doctor. Due to the language problems, many of the people could not accurately describe their symptoms. Without proper examination tools, the exhausted doctor had to prod and probe and make an educated guess at each person's illness. Consequently, many people got the wrong medicine and even if they received the correct medicine, many of them could not read, so they had no idea what it was for or how to take it.

Even under these conditions, those of us who survived began to lead a relatively peaceful life. The Sudanese Christians have always valued education, a well-organized and caring community, and just governance. As soon as we settled in Panyundo, we formed ourselves into a group that met daily under a huge tree to discuss our situation and decide how we would make a future for ourselves. Some of our people had literacy skills and they wanted to start sharing them with the children right away. The Red Cross and UNCHR were very supportive of this, and they introduced us to the English alphabet. We children were determined and eager to learn, so we gathered what cardboard we could, grabbed burnt sticks from the fires for charcoal, and started writing.

This was a good start. The problem was that many of those most eager to show off their skills in literacy, math, history, or geography were not well versed in the skill of teaching. They became very upset when the children did not understand their teaching or when the children did not respond in accordance with their expectations. Sometimes, we children were not sure that these eager teachers really knew what they were teaching, but we allowed them to teach rather than have no lessons at all. After a while, our people built a little schoolroom out of grass, mud, and wood, providing us shelter from the blistering sun. We were determined to focus on what we could do rather than what we could not do. Soon, the Red Cross provided qualified teachers for us, and we were able to make progress in our lessons, even in English.

We began to adjust for the four years that we called Panyundo, Ethiopia our home. We established ourselves in well-constructed houses, schools, and churches. In my church, we conducted Episcopal services where the young people learned the Bible. We had youth programs where the young people participated in the services by dancing and singing. I was almost a teenager by then and was very good at these things. I became one of the leaders for the children's group. We had excellent Bible teachers and preachers who trained and encouraged us as well.

I loved reading the Bible, worshiping the Lord, and singing to God. As I grew older, I began to take part in the activities of the church. Daniel became one of my strong Biblical models as I read about how he submitted himself to prayer and served God even as a captive in a foreign nation.

THE LOST IS FOUND

6

Fleeing to Kenya

In 1990, a group of Ethiopian rebels from the area of Eritrea became discontented with President Mariam of Ethiopia for befriending the Christian refugees from Sudan. These rebels decided to form their own government, which attracted other rebels who were also not happy with President Mariam, mostly because of the refugees who were sharing their land and resources. These rebels began a terrible war against the president. Eritrea's rebel government came into the area of western Ethiopia, where the refugee camp had resettled, to remove the Sudanese refugees by using bullets and artillery. They left thousands dead, and we were told to leave immediately. Even as we began to leave, the rebels attacked us. We again had to flee for our lives from our makeshift homes, with little time to gather our belongings or any food!

When we finally had time to stop and discuss the situation, we were not quite sure where to go. The Arabs occupied the borderlands between Ethiopia and our homeland of Sudan, so we dared not head back in that direction. Our leaders decided to head east to Gilo, a small town on the Gilo River, which was the border between Sudan and Ethiopia.

When we reached Gilo, we were exhausted and stopped to rest. Within seventy-two hours, the rebel militias were following us again, so we fled to the Gilo River. With the rebels right behind us, we had to jump into the river to escape. Since most of us still did not know how to swim, many drowned. The soldiers began shooting at us in the water, then followed us into the river. With their rifles they tried to shove under the water those who were swimming to drown them before they could swim out of reach.

People who could not swim were desperately asking others if they knew how to swim. They wanted to hold onto those who could swim, but we knew that this would result in two people drowning instead of one, so we said we could not swim, even if we could. Once again, a person who knew how to swim carried a rope to the other side so that people could hold onto it while they crossed. Some made it across, but just as before, the bodies and blood of those who did not attracted the crocodiles, and they also took their share of lives. Those of us who made it across had to keep going, running and walking fast in the hot, desert sun. This time, at least we had shoes on our feet and more clothing on our backs.

After many hours of walking, we arrived at Pachalla, a very remote border village with no roads and no available food. There, we managed to subsist on the verge of starvation by foraging for wild fruits for six months. Again, the Red Cross became aware of our plight and delivered food. They soon realized that they too needed help and notified UNICEF (the United Nations International Children's Emergency Fund). These organizations worked together to drop food from the air, saving many lives. Once we regained our strength, we again began clearing fields for activities such as traditional dancing, soccer, and baseball, along with building crude shelters for schools. But we soon learned that our lives were again in danger.

Arab militias had flown to Ethiopia and joined ranks with Ethiopian Muslims who surrounded Pachalla in order to track and kill us! We were attacked on the ground and from the air. Many of our people were killed as we scattered again, running in all directions into the bush. After we reassembled, the UN quickly saw that the bush was also too dangerous for us. They told us to travel to Naarus where they would send supplies.

To get to Naarus, we had to pass through the land of the Magoos, a series of semi-arid deserts overgrown with rough bush and scrub inhabited by very poor people. In this extremely harsh environment, the people have very few resources. They are constantly on the lookout for anyone they can attack, rob, or kill in order to survive. The Magoos proved deadly for us. They killed seven "Lost Boys" and wounded several others. Because no roads existed, we found ourselves aimlessly wandering, not sure in which direction to head for Naarus. We were attacked several times, and more were killed. We arrived at the fairly large city of Capoetia. There we learned that the journey from Capoetia to Naarus was through some of the most remote lands in southern Sudan, which are inhabited by many non-Arab peoples from many different tribes. So, in Capoetia, the UN determined that travel by foot to Naarus would be unsafe for us, and they arranged to drive us. Even though many had been killed, over 16,000 of us were alive, so numerous car trips ensued to get all the people to our destination.

For three months, we lived in Naarus under scrubby trees covered with blankets or whatever we could find. We ate maize, wheat flour, beans, and oil – all supplied to us by the Red Cross. At times, men from the surrounding tribes would bring us meat from their herds to trade for the Red Cross food. We were not sure whether the meat was tainted or diseased, but we craved meat so much that we traded with them.

The Arab militia continued their war against us. They took the city of Capoetia and killed many non-Arab tribal members even though they were not from South Sudan. At the end of the three months, we were told to walk to Loggichogio in Kenya, which is about a day's journey away. Crossing into Kenya, we felt somewhat safer from Arab attack. However, the people who inhabit the borderlands between Sudan and Kenya are some of Kenya's most primitive societies. The Turkanas are the most aggressive of these tribes, especially the men. They are nomads who keep camels and goats as their primary sources of food and income. They attacked us at night and tried to kill us for our possessions, specifically our canteens and clothing. Some of our group were killed, and those who escaped lost their possessions. We also did not realize that the Taposa people from the north were at war with the Turkana people from that area and that we were caught between them. So, for many reasons, the peoples of this area did not welcome a group of sixteen thousand refugees invading their land.

The UN had paid the government of Kenya to protect us. We heard that some police were in the area trying to protect us, but no one could verify that information. At night we formed groups and put our provisions and possessions under a tarp. A group of us would sleep under the tarp while four of us would sit one at each corner to guard our only possessions. If we heard anyone coming we would pretend that some police were close by and call out to them. We were fairly safe by day, unless we went into the bush to gather wood. Then, some people would attack us with big sticks, beat us, or kill us.

7

Kakuma, "The "Nowhere" Camp

After approximately eight months in Loggichoggio, the UN saw that this was not a good place. So they drove us, group by group, to the Kakuma Refugee Camp. In Swahili, the word kakuma means "nowhere." But for us Kakuma was "somewhere." Kakuma was a huge, multicultural refugee camp, which has existed since 1992. At Kakuma, we finally experienced a sort of permanency. The camp was divided into zones. Sudanese refugees had been the first to settle there, followed by Somalians, Ugandans, Burundians, and Rwandans. The UN supplied resources to build schools in each zone. Anyone interested in going to school could attend. Naturally, I was so excited to be able to go to school again!

Living in Kakuma was a mixture of fear and comfort. Although Kakuma provided education, food, and other services, danger still prevailed. The Turkana people did not like us competing for food and resources, so they continued to loot and rob the refugees at night, even in the camps. Food rations were delivered by the UNHCR (the United Nations refugee agency). UNHCR had arranged the refugees into groups numbering up to 100 per group to distribute the provisions, especially water, which was very scarce. Being in a group provided the people with a form of accountability and also gave them connections for social activities, such as sports, theater, or traditional dancing.

I am very good at dancing in the Dinka tradition and also have a good singing voice, so I eagerly joined in the activities. Each group cooked together, got their own provisions in the line, and competed together in sports and other activities. Each person in the group was given approximately two gallons of rations for two weeks. Maize was the most common type of food. It was combined with a few lentils if they were available. This limited supply was not enough to last for two weeks, even though we ate only once a day. People would fight for their share of the rations at the distribution center before they were exhausted by the sun and humidity.

The Kenyan police were deployed around the food centers to keep order, but most of the time, they brutally beat the people when any fights occurred. Of course, very poor sanitary conditions and medical facilities existed, and many of our people died.

Kakuma was a place of extreme poverty unable to offer any way for most people to support their families. These conditions did not stop people from having children, however, and the result was that many small children became malnourished. Those who felt that these were unbearable circumstances went back and forth to their areas in Sudan to get food and other necessities, which was not an easy journey. It was unsafe for the entire group to return to Sudan due to the ongoing war. Any attempt to return as a group would have been suicidal.

The Kenyan police were often hostile and brutal to our people, even though they were paid by the UN to protect us. They would often rob and abuse refugees who were going back and forth to southern Sudan for news and supplies. These officers would take the refugees' money and anything else they were carrying. The police used any kind of illegal means to get supplies they believed to be valuable from foreign travelers, and even from their own citizens. Police brutality, shortage of food, and lack of medical supplies were major threats to our survival.

In spite of the terrible conditions, the directors of the camp did their best to provide a healthy environment for us. They opened sports centers throughout the camp so people could train and complete in basketball and track, and they established a field for wrestling. Traditionally boys and girls are not allowed to mingle, so girls had their separate activities.

We were at Kakuma for nine years. I learned much about people from different cultures and how they think. As a good student, I learned the basics of math, science, English, geography, and the Bible, as well as arts and crafts. Since I was good at socializing and storytelling, I often sat under a lean-to or a shade tree and attracted a crowd of people with whom to talk. I even attracted the attention of some of the girls!

In order for a boy or a girl to get to know one another in our culture, they must go through traditional channels. If a girl wants to get to know a boy, she contacts her friends to help her "set up" a nice place with a table and chairs for a discussion. Then she will send an invitation through a friend to the boy to come drink some water and have a very open conversation with her and her friends. These girls are very smart. As they converse with the boy, they quickly discern if he is insincere or trying to impress her rather than just being who he really is.

My cousins (Majok, Kuai, and Marial), some friends, and I continued to live together in the camp. We rotated the cooking, dishwashing, and the housecleaning chores among us. Each of us took care of washing our own clothes in a bucket. Then, we would hang them outside to dry on nearby trees or a makeshift clothesline. Bit by bit, I learned how to take responsibility for myself. At the same time, I learned to mingle with others and live interdependently. I found that I really enjoyed interacting, encouraging, and helping people. As others responded well to me, I also gained encouragement from them. I very much loved giving gifts, so if I had some little item to give, such as a book, a piece of clothing, or a bit of money, I would give it away with great joy.

When I look back, I understand so much more about the Exodus in the Bible because I experienced an exodus of my own. In the Exodus journey from the Bible, the Israelites walked the desert for forty years with no food to eat and no water to drink, but God provided for them. In our journey as the "Lost Boys" of Sudan, we roamed the desert for forty days from Sudan to Ethiopia with no food to eat and no water to drink. We still experienced God's grace and blessings as he sustained us through very dire circumstances

Despite our strenuous circumstances, we did experience God's marvelous grace in ways that were beyond measure. He protected us from several tribal groups that were all out to steal what little resources we had, and he protected us from others who were determined to kill us all. Though many of us were killed and we were constantly facing attack, God provided the rest of us with shelter, sometimes in a refugee camp or in the bush and he graciously provided us with songs in the midst of our sorrows.

8
Preparing For America

While we were at Kakuma, the Red Cross began the process of locating our relatives. They provided us with paper, pencils, and envelopes instructing us to write a letter to our family members telling them where we were. Then, we were told to put the name of the church we attended, the full names of our relatives, and the name of the state, town, or village where we lived on the outside of the envelopes. The wonderful Red Cross workers then sorted the letters into regions and bagged them up. The bags were taken to the regional churches and given to the pastors, who would then announce that a batch of letters had arrived from Kakuma during church services. The pastors told the congregation they should spread the word so that relatives could come or send someone to the church to help find any letters from missing family members. The Red Cross wanted replies to confirm the letters had been received and to determine which family members were still at home. We were excited to write the letters, and we filled many bags. Several months later, I received a letter back from my family saying that my mother was alive, as well as my brother and sisters. I was so excited. However, little chance existed, if any, that I would ever return to see them, or that they could travel to Kakuma. Still, I was overjoyed to know that they had survived the war.

After nine years, the leaders of Kakuma realized that thousands of young orphan boys and girls were developing with great promise in the refugee camp. But without family connections or any resources, these young men and women would probably never have any hope of making a healthy, productive life for themselves. They did not have access to higher education or resources to learn a skill that would help them secure meaningful work. So, the refugee workers appealed to the UN, specifically the High Commissioner of Refugee Services, to see if something could be done to offer these young and weary travelers a better life. The High Commissioner of Refugee Services consulted with officials of the United States to discuss how they might help with this problem. The United States agreed to bring some of the "Lost Boys" and "Lost Girls" to America. In 1999, the JVA (Joint Voluntary Agency) began a free screening process specifically for the "lost" children of Sudan to make them eligible for travel to the United States. The screening was to verify their correct names and assure that they possessed an adequate ability to function in America and take advantage of its opportunities. That part of the screening proved fairly simple for the workers.

The next step was for the INS (Immigration and Naturalization Service) staff to interview each refugee. This was scary for us because the qualifications included the ability to handle yourself with confidence, speak well, and demonstrate good character and effective people skills. We were advised to look squarely at a person while speaking, even though in our culture such an action is typically regarded as disrespectful. We were told that the judges were strict and that only one-fourth of the boys and girls would pass.

When I arrived for my appointment, my translator began giving me a long list of "dos" and "don'ts" that intimidated me, and included things like don't look down, dress well, speak up, look confident, smile, don't be hostile, and don't be disrespectful. I looked him squarely in the eye and asked, "If the Americans are trying to help us, why are they making it so difficult for us? This has been my home, and if I never get to America just because I do not say what they want me to say, I am not concerned. My ancestors did very well here, and I believe I could also if I had to. It does not seem right for Americans to offer to help us and at the same time put obstacles in our way." My outspoken attitude worried the translator so he tried to calm me. He asked if I really wanted to go to America. I responded that I did not ask to go to America, but America was asking me to come, and they had offered to help me. I told him that with that help, I believed they would see that I get to their country, and that standing one's ground and saying what needs to be said rather than mouthing the words of someone else is always better.

In spite of my strong convictions and my willingness to voice them, I was really scared when I was called into the room for my interview. I had heard that the judges were tough and that if you did not speak carefully, you would fail the interview. The judge asked me to raise my right hand and to tell the truth. He asked me many questions, one of which was why did I want to go to America. I said that I am going to America for better security and better life. Fortunately I and approximately forty others passed the test.

The next step was to go to the International Organization for Migration, where they gave us a thorough physical examination and took our medical histories. After that, they made our travel arrangements and bought our plane tickets. Our tickets cost $850 each, and we had to sign a promissory note to pay them back. They gave us six months to get settled in the United States before we needed to start reimbursing them for our tickets. I was able to pay that sum back well within that time.

9

Arrival in America

Finally, with our tickets in hand, we made our way to board a plane from Kakuma to Nairobi, where we were to finish the paperwork needed for our trip to America. By this time, I was twenty-one years old. I had spent thirteen years of my life with my friends and relatives, walking through deserts and bush land, wearing and washing the clothes on my back, sleeping under trees or in makeshift shelters, living in refugee camps, and eating whatever was available. Now, I was about to board a plane for the first time and fly to the United States of America.

We walked out to the plane in a group, surrounded by some of our friends and relatives from the Kakuma refugee camp. We were all very emotional, crying and saying our goodbyes, not knowing if we would ever see one another again. At about four o'clock in the afternoon, when the sun started to set, we boarded the plane. The plane was small. We were called by name and case number and directed to our seats. We released our emotions by laughing at ourselves as we found our seats. We sat down and fastened our seat belts. None of us knew what to expect.

Then the jets started up. This was the first time since the bombings that we had ever heard such a loud noise. We were not prepared for all the sensations we felt as the airplane began to roll down the runway. Then came taking off. We had just adjusted to the plane being in the air when it began to tilt quite a bit. We looked around at each other with wide eyes; clearly, we were all experiencing the same things. Finally, when we adjusted to the sensation of flying, the plane began to descend, and we felt that our stomachs wanted to lift up and come out of our mouths.

Some were vomiting, some were feeling sick, some had severe headaches, and *all* of us felt our ears stopping up!

We landed safely and boarded a bus that took us to a hotel in Nairobi. On the bus, we began to discuss our feelings. Without the calming influence of our elders or parents, we began to laugh at our friends and ourselves. We joked and poked fun at one another, and each of us expressed our fears about whether the plane would make it or not, whether we had enough gas, whether the loud engines could really get us where we wanted to go, whether our ears would ever work again, and whether our stomachs would ever settle.

At the hotel, we managed to eat a little bit of Kenyan food and then went right to bed. The next day I walked around to explore and found that the hotel was full of refugees from many different areas. The International Organization for Migration had given the cooks money to buy food for the refugees, but we soon discovered that in order to have a little extra money for themselves, they bought the cheapest of foods. At mealtime we were lined up and given a scoop of a corn porridge called *ugali* and a scoop of beans on our plates. Although we were grateful for our food, we certainly missed the delicious meals we had when we cooked for ourselves. It was very cold there at night, so we were glad to have blankets. We were also each given a set of black pants and a long-sleeved pullover shirt so that we would be recognized as a group.

Our next journey was a flight to Amsterdam. By this time we were somewhat more accustomed to the plane, and it was not such a novelty. The plane to Amsterdam was a large KLM (Royal Dutch Airlines), so we were more comfortable. We were really fascinated by the TV screen showing the map of our airplane's route as it progressed. The trip lasted nine-and-a-half hours. I was not familiar with any of the food that was offered on the flight, so I only drank water. Sometimes, one remembers odd things, but I remember too much salad was offered.

This time, we landed at a larger airport. There, we had our first encounter with a moving walkway. We watched how others used it and decided to try it. We laughed and stumbled as we tried to get used to the movement. As we approached the end, we were not sure whether to throw our bags down and hold the rail or just take our chances. We attracted a lot of attention in Amsterdam, and people asked us if we were there to play soccer, since we seemed to be wearing uniforms. After a couple of hours at the airport, we boarded another plane for New York. By now, we felt like experienced travelers.

We arrived in New York at night on March 6, 2001. It was dark outside, but we did not notice because we had walked from the lighted plane, through the lighted loading tube, to the brightly lit lobby. From the lobby, we went to the lower level of the airport to board a bus that was waiting for us. This area was also brightly lit. Suddenly, as the bus left the terminal, we saw it was nighttime. We were so amazed because we thought it was still day.

When we got off the bus, the cool night air blasted our faces like something we had never felt before. We watched in amazement as our breath floated from our mouths and nostrils. I could not even describe what I was feeling because I did not yet have the vocabulary for that in my head. Certain words and phrases cannot be defined until you experience their true meaning! This definitely applies to temperature. I had experienced cold nights in Africa, but they were nothing like the winter cold here. In New York, I experienced freezing cold winter, chilled-to-the-bone bitter cold, and I did not like it.

From the airport, we were taken to a hotel. We began winding down from our long flight and, again, processed all the new sensations that flooded our minds and bodies. We tossed all the new information we had gathered back and forth with each other. Someone told us we could order something to eat. I had no idea what to order, so I pointed to something on the menu I thought seemed tasty. It was shrimp with tails. When it arrived, I told the waitress I could not eat anything with tails. She graciously took it back and gave me another choice. So, I chose chicken, something with which I was more familiar. The chicken was very tasty, probably because it was the first food I had eaten in twenty-four hours. When we got to our rooms, we fell into our beds and slept soundly, like tiny babies.

The next day, we went back to the airport. When we first arrived in New York, we were not used to seeing such big and well-fed people, so we stared, especially at the largest and fattest ones. At the same time, some of them asked us why we were all so skinny. I am sure we must have been an unusual sight - so many very tall, very dark, very skinny people all dressed alike. The Joint Voluntary Agency had put Michigan on my destination paper, but at the airport I was told that my destination had been changed to Houston. I made a big fuss because I wanted to go with my friends, but it was to no avail. I was told I had to go where they sent me, so I was put on the plane with a group that was going to Houston.

10

"Buying Freedom" in Houston

We arrived in Houston around 3:00 p.m. on March 7, 2001. We were taken to the YMCA, the agency that had sponsored us. They housed a couple hundred of us, three to five people to an apartment, and gave us three months free rent. Three other boys named James, Deng, Chol, and I were in one of the largest apartments. The apartments were in a rough, poor neighborhood. The group of tall, very black, Sudanese young men hanging out together and speaking a different language probably appeared very threatening to the people in the neighborhood. When people who speak a foreign language stand around together laughing, it is a pretty common reaction for others to believe that the foreigners are talking and laughing about them. People were not used to our customs, and that caused some problems. In our culture, friends walk together holding one another's hands. Since boys and girls are always segregated, it was just as common for the boys to hold hands with their friends as it was for the girls. In the United States, when we did that, the locals immediately accused us of being homosexuals.

When we sat outside together talking in the courtyard, some of the neighbors heckled us. I spoke to the manager of the Y about the heckling. She told us that they were free to do and say whatever they wanted, so we just needed to ignore them. This was very hard to do. To us, they seemed uninterested in understanding our ways and were simply looking for excuses to curse us and act hostile to us. One of our most pleasant African customs is to hang out together in groups of friends and hold hands. It was natural that we would continue this custom in America, and people looked at us as if we were strange and stupid. I soon learned that it wasn't normal in America for men or women to walk holding hands with the same sex.

Given the communal lifestyle of the African culture, young men hang out together as a symbol of oneness, love, and from a sense of responsibility to one another. However, in America, when young men or women get together out in groups, they are sometimes seen as gang members, which is a very dangerous association.

The importance of Africans staying or living together in groups cannot be overemphasized. In such groups, they discuss their future, how to behave wherever they are, and how to contribute to the development of the society in which they live, whether at home or in diaspora. Groups of young men and women in Africa always have older people who serve as counselors to them. Ten to twenty people can be considered a small group in my culture, given how large one family can be. But in America, a group of ten people might be considered a crowd. That is why such groups would draw the attention of the police. At first, we did not understand why this was unacceptable.

Several times, when we gathered together in Glendale Park as a large group under some trees. the police would stop and question us because they thought we were in a gang. We called the INS office about this, and they sent an agent along with a police officer to sit down with us and explain a little bit about life in America. After that, we traveled in smaller groups that did not appear so menacing, and the police did not bother us. However, reducing the size of our group broke our larger unified fellowship. In our tribes, we were under the constant supervision of elders and authority figures that gave us the support needed to guide our behavior. In America, we were on our own. This breakup of the larger group allowed some to stray into drugs and alcohol, and some copied the negative street behavior they saw.

My first visit to the grocery store was one of the most unusual experiences of my life. I had never entered such a huge building, nor had I ever seen such a huge variety of food. I had twenty dollars which my friends had given me for laundry money. In my mind, I saw America as the source of freedom, and I believed that a huge place like this would surely have the formula for freedom for sale somewhere. I decided to find information about this freedom formula, buy it, and send it back to my people to help them end the horrible war between the Muslims and the Christians in Sudan.

I spent about an hour-and-a-half looking for some sign for freedom, but to no avail. Then, I went to the checkout aisle and asked the cashier if she could help me find something that I was looking for. I told her I was looking for a place to buy freedom. She asked if I were crazy. I was offended.

"What makes you think I am crazy? Do you know me?" I asked.

"No," she answered.

I replied, "I am not crazy and I have money, I am not a beggar, and I cannot find what I want - so I came to you. If you do not know where I can buy what I want, would you recommend someone else who can tell me what I want to know?"

She then apologized and began to listen to me. I explained to her that I came from Sudan, a war-torn country in Africa where many people were being killed, and I believed that the freedom America had would be able to stop the killing. She then explained to me that freedom is not something one can buy. I suddenly realized that freedom is something you have in your heart, mind, and understanding. I began to understand that freedom is a concept. Freedom is first a mindset. When actions that support the concept of freedom are implemented, then, freedom becomes a reality in people's lives.

As far as shopping, I was *really* confused. In Africa, when we shopped, what you saw was what you got. All produce was displayed on tables, shelves, or in crates so you could pick through and choose just what you wanted. The meats and spices were in cases, or hung from racks so you could point to what you wanted. In America, I only saw boxes or packages with pictures and words, which made it hard for me to know what to buy. I had an innate mistrust of packaged and processed foods because I did not know what was inside and how long it had been there. I was used to buying everything fresh. When I drank milk in America, my stomach became upset. I told myself, "Well, I will stop drinking milk." I felt better after that decision. Even learning how to eat certain foods became another challenge.

A few days after we arrived in the United States, two people from the First Baptist Church, who appeared concerned for our welfare, came to visit us. Most of us were Episcopalians, but since we all believe in the same Lord, we felt that we could all work together for the kingdom of God. The Baptists were not the only ones who visited us. After our arrival at the apartments, many people representing many different churches visited us. Our situation with these different people became almost like a garage sale, where things are displayed to tempt people to buy the items whether they needed them or not. The Mormons offered us scholarships; the Jehovah's Witnesses claimed I would be a good Bible teacher and they offered to send me to school. But if we did not agree to *their* terms, their offers were withdrawn.

That Sunday, the same two people from the Baptist Church picked us up and took us to their church. We had never been in such a church. The huge building had a circular design that gave us the feeling of God wrapping His care around us as soon as we entered. We stared up at the video screens that seemed to connect us together with others. We felt surrounded, like we belonged to the community. This was our first exposure to the Evangelical style of worship. Their spontaneous praying, singing, and raising hands impressed me. The dancing and movement in their worship were also very appealing to me. The preacher did not wear a vestment. He did not stand behind a pulpit. He invited people to come forward and pray, which was something I had never seen. All of these practices crossed over the formal division between the clergy and the congregation that existed in the traditional churches I had attended back home. To me, this was a very good, open welcome that connected the clergy and the people together as one, just as God expects of us. The whole service seemed to reflect the moving of the Holy Spirit. Then I heard the passionate words of the preacher and felt God's power. I left the church that day feeling very strongly the power of God.

11
I Regain My Sight

Most of my friends were able to find jobs. I had a more difficult time. When I was a child in Bor, a bad case of measles injured my left eye, which made it challenging to find a job. I consulted with a doctor about having my eye repaired, and he was very helpful. He helped me navigate the Medicaid system to arrange for some surgery. He said that even after the surgery, the healing period would be close to a year before I would be able to work. He wanted to know who would care for me. I said I did not know. The doctor told me to go to the agency that was sponsoring us, which was the YMCA, but they did not want to help. Then I went back to the doctor. This time he gave me a letter and told me to have them sign it, and if they refused to do so, I was to let him know immediately. I took the letter back to the Y and the director saw that she would be reported if she refused. She asked me why I was so insistent. I explained that I would not be able to work for a year and would need to be able to eat. I informed her that if I was in this position in Africa, I could go out to the bush and survive on edible tree leaves and plants, but here in America, I do not know what trees and plants are edible, so what should I do? I told her that if they refuse, then the least they could do was send me back to Africa where I would not starve to death. So they agreed to care for me, and I had my eye surgery.

On May 21, 2001, my cousin and I took a bus to the Memorial Hermann Medical Eye Center in downtown Houston. We arrived at 8:00 a.m. and started the paperwork, which took all morning. It was not until the afternoon that I was ready for surgery. I came out of surgery around 7:00 p.m. and was ready to go home, but we did not have any money for transportation. We went outside and sat on a bench, wondering what to do. After two hours, one of the taxi drivers noticed me with a patch over my eye. He came over and asked us if there was a problem. We explained to him that we did not have any money to get home, so he told us that if we knew the way home, he would take us for free. We were a little suspicious, but he assured us he was sincere, so we went. He took us home, and we were very grateful. I will always be grateful to the American medical system for the miracle of a new corneal transplant and for the generous compassion of that taxi driver. I consider this a sign of God's great grace.

My understanding was that the YMCA agreed to give me the care I needed, but the only care they gave me was a token for the bus to go to the medical center. I thought they had agreed to pay my rent, but as soon as the rent was due, they told me that my roommates must pay my share. The Y had also agreed to provide food for me, but that did not happen either. I was grateful that my roommates shared their food with me. Sometimes, however, none of them would come home in the evening to cook. I was willing to eat whatever they provided, but my dignity prevented me from asking them for food, so I often did not eat any supper. This was an extremely difficult time in my life. I struggled to maintain my dignity until I was on my own, so that I did not leave them with any bad feelings. After nine months, I felt I really needed to find a job so I returned to the doctor in August. I asked to be released because I had to work in order to survive. He agreed, and I was so excited to be able to look for a job.

My first job was in a computer assembly plant with some of my friends. We worked the night shift. On my second night of work, our driver, who was secured for us by the YMCA, picked us up around two in the afternoon to transport us. He was Ethiopian, and we paid him by the trip. On this trip, his girlfriend was in the back seat. He put his music on the radio and kept himself very busy looking back at his girlfriend and talking to her. When we exited the beltway, he reached back to touch her and ran a red light. We hit another car, and the impact rolled our van over three times, breaking all the windows while careening all over the road. No one was wearing seatbelts because the van was over-loaded. My forehead, knees, and neck were injured. That was when we found out that our driver had no license and was not insured. He was a Muslim and spoke very little English. The police asked him what happened. In order not to implicate himself, the driver pretended not to understand English and kept saying to the police *Allahu Akbar* (God is great). Then the police discovered that I could speak a little bit of English, so they began to question me. The officer asked how many were dead. I told him that no one died because God had been with us all the way from Africa and he did not bring us here just to die!

The ambulance arrived, and two of us were sent to Memorial Hospital. The paramedics strapped me to a gurney and secured my neck in case of injury. They kept calling my name along the way to make sure I was conscious. I felt that I was not seriously injured, so I wondered why they were going to all this trouble. When we arrived at the hospital, they rushed my friend and me into the emergency room and cut off our clothes, leaving us in our underwear. They covered us with their paper clothes while they took x-rays and determined that we were okay. After a couple of hours of observation, they released us in our paper clothes, since they had discarded our cut-off clothes. We returned to the apartment for two weeks until we felt ready to return to work. When we tried to go back to work, they informed us that we had lost our jobs.

Not long after that, a lawyer came to visit us at the apartment saying that she had heard about our accident, and she proposed to file an insurance claim against the driver so that he would pay our medical expenses and compensate us for the physical injuries sustained. She was a Nigerian woman who promised us we could collect money for this case because we had injuries. She even sent us to a physical therapist that gave me several sessions of therapy for my neck. A week later, she abandoned us and told us something about not being able to get enough information. We questioned her about why she proposed it and even sent us to get treatment. Of course, we did not get any satisfaction from her and we had to pay all the bills. We also had hospital bills to pay.

THE LOST IS FOUND

12
My Need to Forgive

New events were in play, by the grace of God. I called my friend at the Baptist Church to tell him about the experience with the lawyer. We had a nice conversation, and he invited me to the First Baptist Church to speak to the people about myself and the problems in Sudan. Later, I spoke with Terri, who had heard about me from my friend. He had told her that I was very focused and determined. She asked me what kind of job I wanted, and I said I did not really care. I just needed any job that would pay me, hopefully enough to live. Terri told me she had a heart for the way I talked and she gave me her telephone number. That Monday, I went to her office where I filled out an application, and the next thing I knew, I had a job at Memorial Hospital working in the laundry department. The manager's name was Patrick, and he is a very good Christian man. The majority of the people I worked with were Hispanic and did not know very much English. The job supervisor spoke Spanish, so he could communicate with the workers, but to me he only said "Good" or "No good." It was always difficult to know what was happening! I spoke with the manager about my dilemma. He told me that is how they talk and I was not to worry. I asked him, "If I hear 'no good' what do I need to fix?" Patrick told me that he was impressed with the way I talked so logically and openly to him, and he wondered if I had been some kind of leader in Sudan. After that he called me "Super Jacob."

My friend continued to take us to church. He and others wanted to use our apartment as a gathering place, since it was the largest of the apartments. They wanted to do Bible studies with us and use our apartment for storing and distributing the many items they were collecting for their Sudan relief organization. The Bible studies gave us some good Christian teaching, but we were somewhat fragmented by that time, and not everyone was interested in attending the church. I was one of the older ones most interested in the Bible, so they nominated me to be a youth leader for the Sudanese. I gathered everyone I could and told them they needed to attend the class because we all needed the wisdom of God to guide us. We attended the young singles' classes at church, which would sometimes join the young married class to hear a special teaching or story that they felt would be of value to us. I loved these times of sharing and listening. They were special times of my life. The people in this class reached out to me in a beautiful way. They were interested in what was going on in my life and in Sudan, and often asked me to share about my culture.

One time, after we had shown a DVD about the "Lost Boys," a seven-year-old boy approached me to ask a question. He asked me why the Muslims of Sudan hated the Christians so much. He said his parents had told him many things about this, but he wanted to hear more from me. He wanted me to tell him specifically what I wanted people to do about this situation. I told him to pray for three things: pray for the people, pray for the word of God to reach them, and pray for a peace that would bring them together. The class was giggling about this serious encounter between the little boy and me, but even now, though I do not remember his name, I pray for him in his journey to be a mighty man of God.

It was during this time of spiritual fulfillment that I first heard Billy Graham on TV. I was very impressed. When he preached, my heart was touched by the truths I heard. Graham used his human mind, but he was preaching by the inspiration of God. Through his words, I saw where I needed to change some of my attitudes. During this time, I also heard the wonderful preaching of Joel Osteen from Lakewood Church. The "Lost Boys" went there as a group, and when I heard his preaching, I felt deeply moved because his words had a powerful effect on me. God seemed to be surrounding me with His very own words from so many Christian people that I met and talked with. My heart began to be moved to forgive the Muslims who persecuted us, murdered us, and treated us so cruelly.

When I first came to America, I was angry and felt aggressive toward Muslims, like a man would feel toward a lion that had just mauled him and left him for dead. Changing my belief system was difficult, especially after going through such harmful experiences. Through the power of Jesus, I was able to forgive them just as Jesus commands us to forgive, but I have not forgotten. One may respect the beliefs of others, but that does not mean they have to approve of them. I had read so much in the Bible about how God gives us victories over struggles that I found myself giving my own battle to God for His victory. We might never know how God lets these things happen, but we can know that God is with us in these struggles.

I discovered how differently the people of America think from the people of Africa. At the same time, I understood that much mistrust still exists between peoples of different races and colors, even in America. I realized race or color did not determine how perfect people were, but their thinking and attitudes did determine their paths to holiness. I saw many white people who thought they were better than blacks, and I saw many black people who thought they were better than whites.

In Luke 23:34 (NLT), Jesus looked down from the cross on people of many different races and said, "Forgive them, Father, for they know not what they do!" He was speaking about all of us. After he was resurrected, He promised that He would send the Holy Spirit to everyone who believed. He did not mention whether they were red, or brown, or yellow, or pink, or orange, or black, or white!

When I was in church, united with the white people in worship and prayer, I did not feel separate because I am black. I often felt separated from them when we thought differently or disagreed in our views, but not because of the color of my skin. What I appreciate about Americans is their spirit of kindness and helpfulness. Most of the time, when I talk with people, they try very hard to understand what I want to say. They are very attentive and help me with the choice of my words. I have observed that Americans often smile and give others the chance to speak their piece even when they do not agree. We did not have this kind of support for free speech in Sudan. One did not disagree with the authority figures in our tribe. If a person had a problem expressing himself or herself in our culture, other people would laugh at the person to embarrass them. I also have noticed that most Americans do not get puffed up over their accomplishments and their degrees. These seem to be the positive results of being given the opportunity of free speech. However, it makes me sad when this freedom of speech takes a nasty turn and is used to speak in ways that are harmful. I think I am blessed to have not talked to the arrogant, rude, nasty, manipulative Americans, because they are here too!

Another characteristic I like about Americans is that they care about the poor, the needy, and the less fortunate. Everywhere I look, I see that America is a generous, helpful country. At the same time, everywhere America looks, she sees great need. I think of America as a mother of twins. She does not sleep well because, even though both children are healthy, they both have different needs. She feels responsible to meet both of their needs. I watched so many people respond to the 9/11 tragedy, to the destruction of hurricanes, to the fires in California, to the homeless situation. America is willing to try to solve any problem.

After I had a bad case of measles that affected the retina of my eye, I knew that in Africa, because I had no money, I had no way to get medical help. In America, I was qualified for medical attention, and I received my cornea transplant. I was never asked to pay even a dime, which was amazing. In America, I believe if one has no money, if he or she is sick or hurt and has to go to the hospital, he or she will not be turned away, but sometimes it can happen. Maybe I was blessed by God, since I suffered for a very long time. I lived without good care as a refugee since the age of seven. America generously uses her wealth to meet the needs not only of those on her own soil, but others across the seas who have been victims of war or natural disasters. We will never know the number of people who owe the American people a debt of gratitude. I believe America is led to do this because of strong Christian values. Thankfully, many Americans seem to understand that money can be replaced, but a life lost is gone forever.

At the same time, America, like any other country, is a mixture of people. I have noticed that Americans are very good at smiling, even if they are angry. This seems very encouraging, but it sometimes sends a double message. In Africa, if you are doing bad things, we say right out that you are a bad person or will tell you what you are doing is wrong. Americans seem to avoid this. If we act like everything is okay when something is wrong, then we are possibly denying that person the chance to improve. This does not seem honest. It is better to be honest with the person so that they might change. I once saw the manager at my work pat a man on the back to encourage him when it was known by all of us that this man was not doing his job well. A day later this man was fired. I wondered whether the man could have saved his job if the manager had been more honest with him.

13

On To Pennsylvania

In 2002, I decided I needed more education in order to better serve my people. I chose to attend Houston Community College and was encouraged to do so by many of my friends. I took the SAT tests and tested low in English, but high in math. I was trying to figure out what to do. A counselor at the college suggested I take math since I was good at it, but not English. I suggested to her that I needed English more than math for two reasons. First, without English, I would not be able to understand the math class. Second, I wanted to understand English better so that I could communicate my plans and intentions to my friends. I tend to get very insistent when I am convinced about something, so we had a very intense exchange. She did not appreciate my questioning her judgment. She recommended that I visit and discuss the situation with her supervisor, who agreed with me and calmed me down.. She found an English class for me on the central campus of the college. She registered me into English, math, and reading and sent me to file for financial aid. Of course, like all Americans, I was now in great need of a car, since I would go to school early in the morning and go to work later in the day. The United Methodist Church of Houston donated a car for me to use.

The time it took to travel between school and work consumed most of the time I had to study. One of the professors of my orientation class approached me quietly and told me she was worried about me. When I asked her why, she said she felt I was over-extended and that I might not be able to study enough to pass the courses. I told her I was not worried about failing because passing the classes opened the doors I needed. Failing was not an option. She gave me an approving look and told me to keep up my strong attitude. She said she would pray for me because she felt God certainly had a plan for me. I did manage to finish three classes at Houston Community College. However, I had to withdraw from college to find a better paying job, so I could devote myself to supporting my sister and her three children, who lived with my mother in Africa.

The "Lost Boys" of South Sudan have a very efficient and extensive network of communication among themselves that reaches throughout the United States and to their relatives in Sudan. My cousin and I had been in the Kakuma refugee camp together. Even though he came to the United States after I did and settled with a group in Lancaster, Pennsylvania, I was in constant touch with him. I communicated with him about how overwhelmed I was with the job situation in Houston, and how I needed to find a better paying job. Eventually, he invited me to come to Lancaster because he felt there would be more help for me there. This seemed good, so I took a bus from Houston to Harrisburg, where another friend invited me to stay with him. I found a job in a company called Mac's True Template, which made tools. I worked for one day. The next day, when I eagerly went back, there was a rope barrier with a caution sign across the door. I lifted the rope to enter but a security guard stopped me, saying we were not needed anymore. I asked if complaints about our work had been filed and he said no, they were simply cutting the work force. Then, in my customary honesty, I asked him why they did not cut out his job. He told me I was crazy, but I explained that if there were no workers then there would be no need of security guards. At this he became angry, so I said, "God bless you" and walked away.

I contacted my friends in Harrisburg for a ride home, but none of them had time to collect me. However, they sent a volunteer named John from the Presbyterian Church they attended, who took me to my friend's place. On the way, I shared with him how I lost my job and he was very sorry. I told him not to worry because I believed that when God closes one door he opens another. He answered with a glad *Amen*. I believe he was a bit amazed about my faith, because I seemed to be in such a good mood in spite of losing my job. I admit I was frustrated, but I felt God could give me a job at any moment.

After some time in Harrisburg, I was invited by my cousin to go to Lancaster to stay with him. He felt that opportunities to find a job would be better. When I arrived in Lancaster, I applied to work in the laundry room at Brethren Nursing Home. Because of my experience and good references, I was hired right away. Meanwhile, I continued looking for a better job and applied at Dart Container, where I got a job as a packer.

At Dart, my first assignment was at a station where the machinery moves fast and keeping up with the work is hard. I was new, but before long, I discovered why they put new workers at that machine. Fortunately, my supervisor was very nice. He liked to rotate the jobs so that everyone knew how to do all of the jobs. He partnered me with a woman who exhibited a lot of anger towards me. At first, I could not understand why she was so angry. Then, she told me that her cousin had applied for my job and they had hired me instead. I asked her if she thought I had anything to do with it, since I was not responsible for whom they hired. She and I had some words, and she complained to the supervisor and used some very abusive language to describe me. The supervisor heard my side and decided to get another person to train me. The new person was a very nice lady. I am continually grateful for the people in the workforce who have come to my aid to help me through tough situations.

My cousin attended Calvary Church and invited me to go with him. I looked forward to going back to worship, but before we could go, my cousin's car stopped working, so we had no transportation. We tried to repair the car, but it was too old and beyond repair. That taught us a valuable lesson about buying a used car. That Saturday I was running in the snow, wondering how I could go back to church without a car. I passed a signboard for First United Methodist Church. It read, "Our mission is to introduce people to Christ in a positive way, grow disciples and relieve suffering." That message appealed to me, and the church was within walking distance. So, I decided to attend on Sunday.

In Houston, the "Lost Boys" attended church as a group and the people looked after us with sympathy and compassion. In Lancaster, I walked into the church alone. I was aware that as the only Sudanese person in the church, I would attract attention. I tried to be inconspicuous by sitting in the back and not making eye contact with anyone. I am sure people felt I looked sad because I avoided making eye contact. In my culture, looking someone in the eye is a sign of aggression, and I reverted to my old custom, even though I knew this was not the case in America. After the service, I tried to leave without being noticed, but the ushers were at the doors and one of them reached out his hand to welcome me, and we started a conversation. He asked me where I came from and what brought me to Lancaster. Then he asked about my background, and I shared with him some of my experiences. His interest in me made me feel good.

The senior pastor, Kent Kroehler, appeared and asked me all kinds of questions about my life. I told him about myself, and he made an appointment for me to meet with him on Monday to get to know me a little more. Then he asked if I needed a ride home and I said no, because I only lived three minutes away. Shortly after I arrived home, I received a call and someone wanted to speak with Jacob. It was someone from the church who wanted to make sure I had gotten home safely. I suspected that they also wanted to verify that what I had told them was true.

On Monday, I met with Kent. We talked a long time so he could know more about my story. He was kind and understanding, and I felt very cared for in his office. He called the church staff into his office and introduced me to them. I continued to attend First United Methodist, and they continued to reach out to me. During our meetings, Kent asked me what kind of help I needed for my family in South Sudan. I told him about my two brothers, Ayiei and Lual, who needed money to go to school in Kenya. Kent wired $1,200 for my brothers to attend school. Later, Ayiei had to drop out of school to take care of our mom, but the church continued to pay for Lual's schooling. He graduated from high school and then attended Kampala International University in Uganda. He graduated in February of 2012, with a Bachelor's degree in Social Work.

At church, I also met Bill and Melissa Butler and their son, John. Bill took me to lunch at Pizza Hut, where we got acquainted. He asked me what I wanted to do in my life. I told him I wanted to finish college so I could become a minister. I also told him that I really wanted to get married and have a family, but I wanted a wife from my own culture. I relayed to him how difficult this would be because of the complex immigration process. Bill told me that he had some knowledge in this area and would be willing to help me when the time came. Bill and his family became my dear friends and supporters in the church. I did not know at the time how helpful Bill would later be with the process of my future wife's immigration.

THE LOST IS FOUND

14

Back To Texas

I visited Lancaster Bible College with the hope of enrolling. They said they would not be able to accept me unless I finished my English-As-Second-Language (ESL) classes in Houston. I tried to enroll in the Harrisburg Area Community College (HACC) to do the ESL classes, but they were not equipped to help me. I decided to go back to Houston and finish my courses. When I flew back to Houston, some of my friends met me and took me to the Plantation Apartments in Bellaire, where they were living. I returned to work at Memorial Hospital in the laundry room. They were glad to have me back because they had been pleased with my work. I told them I would still look for a better paying job and my boss said that would be fine.

I registered at Houston Community College's central campus for English, reading, and math. The church paid for my costs, including my books. Transportation was, as always, a problem. The buses to church were unreliable, especially on the weekends, and I would often have to walk two miles to church in the hot sun. I explained to my pastor that sometimes the buses do not run on Sunday. He smiled and said if the buses were not running it would be all right to stay at home. I told him I wanted to be with God's people on Sunday, and that we were forced out of our country because of our commitment to God. I was not going to allow a transportation issue to keep me from church in America! He patted me on the shoulder to encourage me.

God provided me with a donated Pontiac Bonneville which made it easier to get to college and church. I was delighted to find that the College of Biblical Study offered scholarships for the "Lost Boys." After I finished my courses at the Community

College, I enrolled at the College of Biblical Study and was able to finish fifteen courses with them.   Now that I had a car, I enthusiastically joined in the activities of my new church.   I attended the singles Sunday school classes and joined the choir, because I really wanted to sing to the Lord. Even though I did not know the songs very well, I gave my best. One time, a friend who stood next to me said, "I don't hear you." I told him that I sing for the Lord, not for him.

Another friend, Nancy Dumas, invited me to a birthday party for her husband, Jerry. At this time, I had never been to anyone's home before in the United States, and I was excited to see how birthdays were celebrated in America. I could hardly believe that the most respected CEO in my church had invited me to a party. After work, I went home as if I were floating on clouds. I could hardly wait! Jerry arranged for me to be picked up by one of the Sunday school members. We drove through the beautiful grounds around a golf course to a splendid country club building. Inside, the rooms were richly decorated in gold draperies and elegant trappings.   Waiters were everywhere, offering trays filled with beautiful food and delicious pastries, along with all kinds of drinks. The huge room was filled with people, and I felt as if Jerry introduced me to all of them. They shook my hand and asked me what company I owned or worked for, or asked if I had met Jerry on a business trip. I answered that I met him at the Lord's house. I met some of my Sunday school friends, and they were as excited as I was about the party. I had never tasted such rich, delicious food, and I had never had the opportunity to talk with so many different people.   I was greatly amused when I realized that everyone there expected me to own a business or to be some sort of executive. Afterward I asked Jerry why they asked me that. He said not to worry, some day I was going to own something. That gave me a lot to think about.

The next Sunday, Jerry, who taught our singles' class, sat and talked to us about the party. We expressed our gratitude about being invited, and he answered that the gratitude goes to God, not him. He talked to us about being wealthy and serving God. He told us how broke he was before he built his business and said that we all had as much access to God's help as he did. He even told me that having me in Sunday school inspired him to draw closer to God. His humble heart, in spite of his power and wealth, blessed us all.

Jerry said that, as a Sunday school teacher, he saw that I had a calling from God. I had considered joining the U. S. Army because I wanted to fight the Muslims who had caused me so much grief. Jerry said he felt that joining the army would divide my heart in a way that would detract from God's calling. He saw that my contributions in class, along with what he had heard from the church people when I visited the local prisons, showed my strong calling as a man of God. He felt that my talents would not be effective in the military, because if I were sent to Kenya or to Egypt, what could I do for the people and how could I speak for God? He said that if I trained for God's army, I would be free to go wherever God sent me. He felt God could achieve great things with me because I was called at such a young age.

From the moment we first arrived in Houston as immigrants, our custom among the Sudanese group was to fellowship together for church on Sundays. When we first arrived, many of our people were fellowshipping in one of the larger apartments open to us. The apartment became too small. In 2001, we approached the Presbyterian Church in Bellaire to see if we could use their fellowship hall. This church already had some Sudanese members, so they were more than happy for us to use their facilities. We called our congregation the Sudanese Community Church because our Sudanese group was multi-denominational. We met in the Presbyterian Church fellowship hall every Sunday at 2:00 p.m. I enjoyed these times very much. We were together as Sudanese, and I was asked to be in leadership. Now, I was a pastor, and there we were praying and encouraging one another in our native tongue.

I was in Houston from March of 2002 through 2005. I spent the next couple of years reflecting on my life. I had a job, an apartment, and was well-settled in America. The time was right to go visit my mother, my family, and to get married. When I mentioned to Jerry that I would like to return to South Sudan, he knew that I would need to make more money to finance my trip. He offered me a job with his oil refining company, Flotek, in Midland. When I discussed it with a friend, he was concerned. He said that I would probably have a hard time fitting in with the workers because of their attitudes, and he advised against it. At the same time, my friend said that if God led me to try it out, I could always come back if it did not work. I decided to try to make it in Midland, so Jerry made all the arrangements.

In 2005, I left my roommate in charge of the apartment in Houston, and I moved to Midland, Texas to start the next chapter of my life. The manager of Flotek met me at the airport and took me to a hotel where Jerry had arranged for me to stay. I had no idea where this hotel was in relation to my job, but they arranged for a supervisor to deliver me to and from work. A restaurant was conveniently located next door to the hotel, but I did not particularly enjoy their food. I wondered how they could make meat taste sweet. I was unfamiliar with the area and having to find my way around was depressing. One day, I called a Yellow Cab to take me to Wal-Mart, so that I could at least be in familiar territory and buy what I wanted. I went there every week. Looking back now it is quite strange to think of Wal-Mart as a place of comfort, but it was for me at the time.

The hotel was not very clean and had a severe bug problem. I made multiple complaints to the managers, but it took them quite a while to respond. After some time, they finally moved me to the first floor. This was a very difficult time for me. I wondered what I was doing in Midland. Why did I move here? Why did I give up all I had in Houston for a hotel room that made me uncomfortable? I wanted to give up and move back, but I stayed for six weeks to work and save money.

One time, while I was waiting in the checkout line at Wal-Mart, I saw a mother with her two children, a boy about ten and a little girl about three. The mother asked the little girl to take her brother's hand. She obviously liked her big brother and reached out to him, but he refused and said a very emphatic, "NO!" The little girl began to cry. The mother took her hand and asked the boy to go and get some bread off the shelf for her. Again, he gave an emphatic, "NO!" I was amazed at the son's reactions because in my culture this is looked upon as disrespect. Our children are taught at a young age that they are to be respectful, regardless of how they feel. Any disrespect is corrected immediately with some sort of unpleasant consequence. When they are very young, it might be a firm hold on the arm to remove the child from something he wants, or a firm spanking on the hand or leg, or it might be a very stern voice and look. When they are older, the punishment might be several hours of separation from their friends, going all day without food, or the deprivation of something dear for a period of time. Grandparents, aunts, uncles, and elders all contribute to the parental training since we live in close communities. A child hears many lectures from all of them. This arrangement provides accountability for the child and much support for the parents. Until I saw this scene at Wal-Mart, I was not aware that many American parents do not have that kind of support from their families, and often they have no role models or any experience to provide proper training for their children.

In my innocence, I approached this little boy and asked him why he did not help his mom. He looked at me in utter surprise. I continued by asking why would he come shopping with his mom if he was not going to be helpful. He answered that he didn't want to do anything. So, I helped his mom get the bread and asked her what else she needed and helped her get those things also. She thanked me. I faced the little boy and told him that he was not to eat any of the bread or other things his mother had just bought. He asked me why not. I told him that since he did not help his mom or his sister, why should he be able to eat with them?

His mom then told me that when I first spoke to her little boy, she was upset. She said that in Midland a black person would not dare speak to a little white boy, much less correct him. However, she said that when she heard my accent she knew that I was not accustomed to this culture, and when she heard what I was saying, she realized I was not crazy but speaking real wisdom. She liked what I said and thought it might teach him a lesson. I told her I would pray for her. Her large cart was totally full and would have been very difficult for her to manage with two little ones, so I pushed her cart out to the car. She said she would put this experience in her diary and would also pray for me.

The afternoon was very hot. I helped her load her groceries into the car, then pushed the cart back to the corral. I was very sweaty as I walked back to say goodbye and ask God to bless her. She pulled out a five-dollar bill to pay me. I refused the money, saying it was because of God that I helped her, and I wanted my witness to be sincere. She continued to press the money on me and even called a nearby fellow over to try to talk me into taking it. He tried very hard to convince me, but I said I did not want to take it. What I did came from my heart, and to take money for it would rob both of us of God's blessing. He said I should take the money. When I still refused, he said it was the first time he ever heard of such a thing. I said he may never have heard of it, but in my experience many people out there would do the same thing. I told him maybe he should not limit himself only to people who would take money and get to know more people who would do similar actions. I suggested that if he thought so much of getting this money, maybe he should take it. He left, throwing up his hands.

The mother smiled at me. This experience gave me a glimpse of how the fragmentation of American families has robbed parents and children of the community support that we have in our tribal culture. I took a cab home with my frozen food for the microwave. I had been in Midland for two weeks and was beginning to feel a great deal of frustration. I had no transportation, and my life consisted of my manager bringing me back to the lonely hotel room every night.

15

My Life in Midland

While I was walking to the nearby restaurant one day, a police officer screeched his car to a halt on the opposite side of the road and hurried across to talk to me. He asked me where I came from. I told him I was from Houston and had a job at Flotek. He asked me where I lived. I told him the hotel. Then he asked me if he were to go into the hotel, would they know me. I assured him they would. Then, I asked him why he was giving me the third degree. Was it because he knows everyone in Midland and I was the only stranger around, or does he do this to everyone in Midland? He said he did not do it to everyone, but it was how they looked for drug dealers. I asked him if I could have his badge number and if he would give me a paper stating that he had stopped me and found that I was not a drug dealer, so I would not have to go through this again with another policeman who thought I looked suspicious. He started to laugh, but he flipped his badge over so I could not see it as he turned and hurried for his car. As he left, I waved and thanked him for alerting me about how I would be treated in Midland.

When I left Houston, the United Methodist Church there had written a letter for me to deliver to Pastor Terry at First United Methodist in Odessa, a city attached to Midland. However, when I called Pastor Terry, I discovered that they had given me the wrong phone number. I had to call back to Houston for the right number, and they took over a week to return my call. I really wanted to go to church, so I asked one of the desk clerks at the Inn if they knew of any United Methodist churches in Midland. They gave me a phone book and said I could probably find what I wanted in the yellow pages. I found the phone number for a

United Methodist Church in Midland and called them. I told the church receptionist that I was a United Methodist church member and was new in the area. The church had no transportation to help me, so I called a cab after work one day and asked him if he would take me there. I wanted the cab driver to go along the bus route so I would know where to catch a bus. He told me he would be glad to do that, but it would add to the cost. I agreed to the cost, and he was very helpful along the way and pointed out all the bus stops for me.

That Wednesday evening, I went to a church in Midland and met with the senior pastor. He asked me many questions about myself and said he would be happy to have me in his congregation. The church was huge. When I went into the sanctuary, I sat in the middle of one of the large pews, so that if anyone wanted to sit beside me they could. By this time my perspective was more advanced, and I did not expect anyone to sit with me, and no one did. A woman named Glenna was very helpful and arranged for the church to give me a chance to show a tape about the "Lost Boys" at Sunday school. I presented the video twice, but I had very little experience concerning presentations and people felt uncomfortable approaching me. I also joined the choir to get to know more people, but no one showed much interest in me despite all of my efforts at friendliness.

One Sunday after the service, I was sitting by myself in the pew. As I got up to leave, a man approached me and asked me why I kept coming to "our" church. I was puzzled by his question. He informed me that nobody liked me. I asked him what he meant. He said he did not want to talk about it. I asked him if he knew what the church was really all about. He answered that he did not care. I asked if he thought Jesus was American by birth, or by naturalization. When he asked me why I said that, I told him that if he did not accept me because he thinks I am a foreigner, why would he accept Jesus? By then other people started to gather around us. They began to defend me and argue with him. They assured me that no one agreed with him, and that he had some mental problems. The experience was not pleasant, but I was happy that other people in the church defended me, so I kept attending.

While I was in Midland, I wanted to continue my college education. I began the enrollment process and the college sent for my transcripts from Houston. However, I could not get enough money to finish my enrollment, so I had to drop out. The college sent back the six hundred dollars. At the same time, I was sad that I could not go to college. I was also frustrated with my room at the hotel because they had discovered bedbugs and had to move me. Dealing with the run-down hotel was wearing on me. Also, I was tired of eating at the same restaurant. Nothing seemed to be working for me. I felt frustrated, lonely, and unhappy.

I finally received a phone call from Houston giving me Pastor Terry's correct phone number. When I got in touch with him, he and his wife, Vicki, were wonderful to me. They took me to a grocery store and a nice restaurant. They also took me to their church. I had saved enough money for an apartment, but no one would rent to me for cash. Terri and Vicki graciously went with me to get an apartment and used their credit card. That opened my choices tremendously. After I found an apartment, I needed furniture and other help, but Christmas was arriving, and everyone was very busy.

One day, a small group headed by a woman named Linda asked me for the keys to my apartment so they could do some work in it for me. I was surprised by their request, but gave them the keys. I did not know that they had arranged for furniture to be donated through a local store. When I came home from work that night, my apartment was fully furnished. This greatly blessed me and made things feel more like home. I wanted to continue with the Odessa church, but it seemed to me that I should not add to Pastor Terry's work schedule by needing constant transportation to and from his church, which was about forty-five minutes away.

In Midland, I was still in great need of transportation. Some friends arranged for me to get a car. It was a huge 1996 Oldsmobile and monster cars were not something to which I was accustomed!

A short time after buying the car, I went to the Midland Department of Public Safety (DPS) to have the address changed on my license. They informed me that I had a class B license, which was only a learning permit. That meant I had never taken the road test. Also, my car had a light out and I could not use it for a road test until it was fixed. Since I only had a learning permit, I could not drive the car off the property.

I called Glenna, my friend from the church in Midland, and she sent a friend to take me home. I told her my problem, and she said I could use her car for the test. I called a friend to drive me back to the DPS in Glenna's car, but the situation actually went from bad to worse. When we arrived with Glenna's car, they discovered that her sticker had expired. When they asked for the insurance card, we discovered that her insurance had expired. I could do nothing but just smile and ask what I should do now. By this time, they had some compassion for me and allowed us to take the car home. They advised us that if we got a ticket on the way, we could probably take care of everything that same day and the ticket would be cancelled. When I got home, I called Glenna again. She told me to go to her husband's workplace and he would give me his credit card and we could get everything done. At that point, I decided to fix the light on my own car and use it to take the test.

I arrived at the DPS with my big old Oldsmobile. The lady running the test looked rather intimidating in her uniform and very dark sunglasses. She had me test all the emergency lights before proceeding. When we started driving, she began telling me little things I was doing wrong like hitting the brakes too hard, going 50 mph in a 45 mph zone, and other annoying but necessary information, which distracted me. I finally asked if she could please tell me later since I was trying to concentrate on driving. Needless to say, my remarks, which I now know were out of line, annoyed her, and this made me even more nervous. When we finished, she told me I needed to practice some more and would have to come back. In spite of her annoyance, she was gracious. Two days later when I returned, I finally passed the test.

In March, my friend Suzy asked me to speak at an event called Teen Challenge. She made the arrangements and accompanied me, as I really had no idea what Teen Challenge was. Upon our arrival, we met the director. I showed my 60-minute "Lost Boys" video and shared some of my difficult experiences. Afterwards, many of the young people approached and shared with me. They said they had thought it was hard when their parents asked them to help around the house, but after seeing my tape, they had a better understanding of real hardship. They asked me why the people treated us like that in Africa. I told them it was because we stood for Christ and for our freedom to practice Christianity. I told them that real freedom is not freedom from rules and regulations, but is freedom to stand for God's principles of justice and freedom to worship him. I told them that we need the wisdom of God to fight intelligently for true freedom.

After the meeting, new help arrived in the form of an unexpected gift. A person whom I didn't even know left me a check for $400. Also, on March 20, 2005, Suzy set up a meeting with the US Representative for both Odessa and Midland, so I could share the concerns of the "Lost Boys of Sudan" in Africa and America. He sat very quietly and listened carefully to what I said. He asked me how I became a Christian and what I planned to do when I went back to Africa. He also shared that he and his family were Christians. Suzy pointed out to him that I was wearing a t-shirt that said "New Sudan" with the new flag displayed on it and that she was wearing a t-shirt with the American flag because she felt that America should work with those who are fighting for democracy in Sudan. He told me he would try to help in any way he could. At the end of our meeting, I presented him with an African shirt, which a relative had made and sent to me. He said that in his position he was not allowed to accept gifts, but that he would be happy to buy the shirt. This impressed me because bribery is so prevalent in Africa that no one thinks anything of it. After having our picture taken, he asked if he could pray with us. His prayer was very eloquent and meant a lot to me.

I had been in touch with Kent about my unpleasant experience with one of the churches in Midland, and he told me he wanted me to go to St. Luke's United Methodist, which was very close to where I lived. He assured me that it would be a much better church experience. After speaking with Kent I received a call at my work from Pastor Richard of St. Luke's saying he had spoken with Pastor Kent, who wanted me to visit his church that evening after work. Richard was very hospitable, and I began to attend his church. He made sure to welcome and introduce me to people so that I was not wandering around alone. He let me show my "Lost Boys of Sudan" video, which generated much interest.

My friends from Houston had also told me about the Stone Gate Church, which had a huge outreach program in Sudan and had sponsored one of the "Lost Boys." One night I went with Suzy to a concert at that church. They had colored lights, a big screen, great music, and I got caught up in all the excitement and prayer. With the vibrant programs and good music, the church was growing fast. I really enjoyed the services whenever I went. This was one of the highlights of my church life in America, because it was the first time I felt the people were looking at me as a fellow Christian rather than as a black person from Sudan. I will always remember that congregation for having integrity on that point.

Meanwhile, I was learning much at work. My first day at the Flotek plant, my manager introduced me to the supervisor, who took me on a tour of the plant. Afterwards, my supervisor turned me over to the man who would be my boss. He asked me what I wanted to do in the company, and I told him I wanted to learn how to cut pipes. He faced me squarely, and I could see that that was not going to happen. He informed me that I was going to clean floors like my "brother" and pointed to a black man cleaning floors. As this was my first day on the job, I agreed.

The next day, my boss gave me a pick ax and told me to go out back and cut the grass. The grass was taller than I was, and of course a pick ax is not the proper tool for the job. When I informed him of this, he said that if I didn't cut the grass, I would be fired. He wanted me to react in such a way that I would quit. I decided I would not quit but would force his hand, so I stayed out in the grass until quitting time. In the morning, he put me to work cutting the trees outside. After that, he told me to clean the floors with my "brother." I was happy to do this because it was a public witness to the others that I was willing to do whatever I was given to do. Meanwhile, my boss continued to badger me. However, the other workers soon tired of his unfairness and told him to "back off." One day, the manager came to where I was working and asked me about the situation with my boss. I explained my side of the story, and the manager said he would talk with the boss. After that, my boss left me alone. Two days later, the manager had a meeting in his office with the two of us. My boss apologized in front of the manager, so I thought things were resolved. However, my boss was not yet through with his agenda. Over the following few weeks, other things happened. Even the other workers were getting upset with him. At one point, I became extremely angry, and he became frightened that I might hurt him. He asked me not to beat him because he had a wife and four children. I asked him if he spoke to his wife and family using the same words that he used with me, and he said no. Then I asked him why he used such words here. He did not answer. I did not have to go back to work the Monday following our argument, but someone from the manager's office called and told me to come for a meeting with the manager, the general manager, and the human resource person from Houston. During the meeting they asked me to tell them my side of the story. After hearing it, the human resource lady demanded that the boss be fired. I told her that if she fired him I would quit also. Surprised, she asked me why. I told her that to fire the man would only perpetuate the problem. It would be best to re-educate him. They agreed and called him in to speak with him. He signed a paper that said he would neither cuss nor disrespect the workers. They told him that I was a religious man, and he had no right to treat me the way he had. Then, he and I shook hands.

I worked for another couple of months with the company, and he was friendlier to me. When I left Midland, he made a point to approach me to say goodbye. He told me that I was the best worker he ever had, and he never knew a black person could work like that. Then he said that I was a strong and kind person. At the same time, he confessed that he was still not able to overcome his prejudice against black people. I told him that I did not hold it against him since it was probably his mindset of many years, but that I myself am able to look at a person as a person, regardless of their skin color.

16

Reunion in South Sudan

Before leaving Flotek, I made arrangements to go see my mother in South Sudan. When my brothers and sisters heard of my plans, they were very happy. At this time, I was twenty-five years old. After more than seventeen years of separation, we were extremely excited to see each other. I had saved enough money to buy my ticket and cover all of my expenses for the trip. The time arrived to complete my paperwork. The first step was to get traveling documents. After that, I bought my ticket, and got all of my immunizations. I had to send all of the travel information by overnight mail to the Uganda Embassy in Washington, D.C., and in two weeks they sent me a visa. I gave two weeks notice at work and to the apartment owners. I put my furniture in storage in Odessa, left my car with a friend at church, and flew back to Houston.

When I arrived in Houston, I called Nancy and Jerry to tell them I was ready to leave for South Sudan. Jerry made arrangements for me to meet him at Westchase United Methodist Church. We hugged each other when I arrived. He told me that his company had reported that I did such a good job and worked so hard that he felt I had earned the money for the car, so he did not want me to pay it back. We were very emotional when we said our goodbyes.

As the date of my flight arrived, I became very excited at the thought of again living in my own culture and seeing my family again, especially my mother. I was not sure what to expect. I was only seven years old when I last saw my mother and my village. I knew nothing would be the same, but the love of a family and one's relatives never stops. I was eager to embrace them once again. I was eager to hear their stories and to tell them mine. As the elder son, it felt good to send my mother and my relatives some support money. Now, I not only could take them extra money, but would be able to hold them and give them my love as well. Just going to the airport and getting on the plane filled me with so much joy that I wanted to shout to everyone that I was going to see my family.

I left Houston on April 27, 2006, and flew to Amsterdam and then to Entebbe Airport in Kampala, the capitol of Uganda, on April 28th. My brother, Ayiei Guot Ayiei, and sixteen other relatives who lived in Kampala met me in the airport. We all hugged and jabbered while we got the luggage together and then boarded a van. Culture shock hit me when we all piled into the old, rickety van without air conditioning. Even the oldest car I had in the United States did not shake and rattle like this van. I asked my brother if this was the last thing on the rental lot, and he replied that I should remember I was back in Africa, not in America. I began thoroughly enjoying life the "African way" again. After my four days in Kampala, I felt that I had reconnected.

My brother went with me from Kampala to Nakuru, Kenya. In Africa, taking a bus is a totally different experience than in the United States. You are never quite sure how long a trip will take. The bus often makes unscheduled stops for people who flag you down, and it takes time to load and unload possessions on top of the bus. When we reached the border, we all had to get off and file into a room for an official border check. When the officer reached my brother and me, he asked to see our papers. My brother showed him his papers from Sudan. I did not yet have my citizenship from America, so I had been given a traveling document from Sudan that I showed to him. The officer told my brother he could go through, but my traveling papers were not valid and I would have to pay to cross the border. I was convinced that he had recognized my American accent and was trying to get money from me. I was willing to pay, but my brother refused, saying the papers were valid. We were taken into a very dark room and were questioned by a guard who shined a flashlight in our faces. We stayed there four hours trying to get through, but the officer insisted I pay, and we finally did. I could have saved my brother a lot of time if he had let me pay immediately.

In Nakuru, we visited some more relatives. We were there only a few hours when we learned that one of our cousins had been in a car accident and was in the hospital in Nairobi. We immediately went to Nairobi in a taxi to visit and comfort him. His wife arrived while we were there, so I got to meet her as well. My cousin's injuries were very serious. In our culture, we are comforted when surrounded by many caring people. We stayed there two hours, and then returned to Nakuru. From Nakuru, we left for Loki, a small and remote town. We would later rent a little plane to fly to my village in Bor. In Loki, I reconnected with some friends from the Kakuma refugee camp, and we had a very emotional time together. I had the honor of buying dinner for all of us.

We went to the little airport in Loki every day, trying to get a flight to Bor. The airport had a small ticket office, but no sales people, no schedules, and no prices! Tickets are sold through dealers, and one never knows whether his prices are fair or not, or whether the tickets will be valid. After buying a ticket, the passenger does not know the schedule of the tiny plane. We had spent five days in Loki, and since my brother and my cousin were traveling with me, I felt obligated to pay all their expenses.

Finally, we were able to buy our tickets to leave at five in the morning. We saw a tiny, single engine airplane with two ropes helping to hold its wings to the body. I asked the person who sold us the ticket where that little plane was going, and he said that it was our plane to Bor. I began to worry, even before we got on the plane. The ticket agent assured us that this old, tiny plane was one of the more reliable ones. When we boarded the plane, I asked the pilot if he thought we would reach our destination. I told him that the ropes worried me and wondered why the wings had to be tied to the plane. He informed me that the ropes stabilized the wings, and did more than just hold them to the body. Nine of us boarded, and someone came out of the little ticket office to hand push the propeller. I was not sure the plane would get off the ground, but it finally did, and after four anxious hours, we landed in a field in Bor.

We arrived in the rain, and as soon as I got off the plane, I immediately knelt on the ground and gave thanks to God. The people surrounding me wondered why I fell on my knees in the mud while wearing a clean, new suit. I told them I was praising God for his mercies to me and for bringing me back to my country. I was seeing and touching my native soil again, and I was with my mother, my friends, and my relatives, all of whom I had not seen for all these years! Soon, my sister and many other relatives came to us and picked up our bags. We all began to walk to our village. There, I finally greeted my mother, aunts, uncles, cousins, and friends. I hugged each and every one of them. What an indescribable moment for me!

Jacob and his mother, Akon Ayuen Kuany

The next morning, members of my family and tribe surrounded me. We were laughing and crying with joy. To celebrate my homecoming, my family slaughtered a bull. My mother motioned for me to sit in her lap so she could feel my presence as the child she did not get to nurture. I said I was no longer that child and she might regret it if I tried to sit on her lap. But, I actually did gently settle myself onto her lap, because I felt her need for some closure. That evening, my relatives and friends staged a special dance for me. Their exuberant movements to tribal music in brightly colored clothing, celebrating according to our tribal customs, brought back so many exciting memories to me.

After the dancing and fellowship, we all gathered for the wonderful meal. A rich array of aromas, color, movement, action, and sounds all flooded into my brain. I felt overwhelmed with joy. During the meal, I met with the elders, and we exchanged our greetings. I was permitted to sit with them while I told them about my experiences, and they told me what had happened to them during all those years I was gone. Late in the evening, my parents organized a big prayer session for me. They thanked God for saving me in the wilderness, for giving me the opportunity to go to the United States, and for reuniting us. After prayer, most of the people departed, leaving me with my parents and some of the closest leaders from the Payam of Jalle. Our time together was sweet and intimate.

THE LOST IS FOUND

17
Dinka Marriage Customs

Before my arrival to Sudan, I had told my mother that I wanted to marry a woman from my culture. Many people in the United States had suggested that I find an American wife, but in my heart I knew that would not be for the best. I felt a calling to be a pastor to my people in Sudan. In order to minister to them in a meaningful way, I would need to have a wife who understood and was intimately connected with the culture. An American woman would not be able to minister to the women in Bor. Of course, my parents were happy for my decision. Marriage is such a huge event in our culture. As soon as my parents heard of my desire to marry, they immediately alerted the elders of my family so they would have time to consider my request and begin the process.

Marriage is regarded as the most valuable institution among the Dinka people. Marriage is considered not only a union between a husband and a wife, but also the joining of two families. Divorce is rare. It is viewed as a moral failure and brings shame to a family. When a man has great wealth and can provide for more than one wife and family, a polygamous relationship can flourish. The Dinka people accept the practice of polygamy since it was accepted in the Old Testament, and it had been their custom since their history began in the 1400s.

The wives must respect one another, the husband, as well as all of the children. The children are taught to respect their stepmothers and their step-siblings as well as their father. The husband builds houses close together for each of his wives, and the children can live in any of the homes based on where they are most comfortable. The wives generally come together and help one another collectively during times of heavy work, such as cultivating, planting, harvesting, and special celebration ceremonies. The wives also help one another in times of childbirth and sickness. It is the duty of the wives to teach their children to love each other and care for one another. The father allocates and assigns resources and responsibilities to the elder sons and daughters of the marriage. The elder children become, more or less, the pioneers of the family, determining the kind of life and relationship that will follow for the rest of the children. The elder children see to it that their younger brothers and sisters are properly washed, that their milk containers are kept clean, and that they behave properly.

Families are known by their reputations. It is the responsibility of the fathers to provide for their families. In particular, they needed to provide training for their boys to be responsible men and their daughters to be kind and capable women. In addition, the fathers make sure their wives have their needs met, so they will not cause discord within the family. Since respect holds the whole community together, to disrespect your elders in the Dinka culture is a serious offense which can bring a curse upon yourself and your family. Disrespect can also result in severe discipline, such as additional work duties or even the denial of food for a day. The tribes take pride in the making of beautiful canes from various types of wood or bamboo, and they are treasured possessions of the men of the tribe. Occasionally, a child who misbehaves will feel the sting of one of those canes on his or her back. The elders have greater powers to exercise over the children, but if the elders abuse those powers, they lose respect in the whole community.

A husband must make sure that all the wives and children are given a fair share of the family's resources. An older wife is usually given the responsibility of assisting the husband in family matters. The first wife sits with the husband to discuss how milk should be allocated. The husband also seeks her input in considering any new arrangement in the family, such as a marriage, the selling of a cow for money to send the children to school, the handling of sickness or an outbreak of hunger.

The children of each village grow up in the fellowship of their peer group. The boys grow up building friendships through wrestling, fighting, joking, dancing, singing, and games, which provide all kinds of socializing opportunities. They even eat together as a group. The influence of the group helps them to be on their best behavior so they gain the respect and admiration of their peers. In their individual peer groups, the boys and girls also correct each other, helping to mold good character in one another.

Boys and girls never interact socially. The boys herd the animals, and learn farming skills and business negotiation. The girls work at home with the women, learning to cook, care for babies and the home, and provide food and hospitality for family and community gatherings. When the sons or daughters have reached a certain stage of maturity, they are initiated through certain rituals, like my scarring, which are held periodically. People from the village as well as relatives from other villages join the celebrations.

The father has to buy his child the cultural attire and ornaments for the initiation, and for this, he uses cows, which are the main source of wealth. These initiation gifts include elephant tusks, leopard skins, drums, ostrich feathers, spears, bangles, and ornamental sticks and canes made from ebony and bamboo. After initiation, the person is considered mature and is given more responsibilities in the community. When these elder children grow to maturity, they might pass on their traditional attire to their successors.

A son receives a beautiful Mariar or Majok bull from his father. These bulls are specially cultivated and trained, and such a bull is worth many cows. A Mariar or Majok bull is required by the family of a bride as a gift from the groom. So, this gift from the father to the son is very important. The elder son has the first priority to marry, and the rest of the sons must wait in turn depending upon their position in the family. The father must also consider the number of bulls and cows to provide for a marriage dowry. The dowry varies depending on the economic level of the family. Sudanese cultures beside the Dinka use money or treasure for a dowry, but the Dinka culture continues to use cows for a dowry. The dowry shows honor to the girl's family, so it must be done delicately. In the Dinka culture, the groom pays bulls and cows to the relatives of his bride, starting with the father, who gets the most cows and probably a prize bull or two. The bride's mother gets a number of cows. The oldest brother, who has had the responsibility of carefully watching after and protecting his sister as she grew up, gets a Mariar bull, and then the girl's uncles get progressively fewer cows according to their birth order. Perhaps a cow or two will go to very important members of the girl's extended family.

Most marriages cost in the range of thirty cows, but some might go for fifty or even up to 150 animals if competition exists for a particular girl. In the pastoral communities of South Sudan the cows are considered wealth, and the primary way of acquiring many of them is through marriage. These cows are the major means of survival and are extremely important to the family. Many cows died in 2006 during the war. Their death had a devastating effect upon our people. Without cows, the people are deprived of milk, meat, and ways to make their living. Male children can marry only if they have their own cows.

After the cows have been paid to the family of the bride, the wedding is secured and must be carried out. In the tribal cultures, the children of the marriage are considered to belong first to their father, since he has paid many cows for their mother. This ownership of the children ensures that the wife stays with him permanently. The giving of a dowry is a way for the people to keep the wealth circulating in the community from generation to generation.

It is not an easy task to bring up a girl who is fully skilled in running a home, caring for children, and being a responsible wife, so she will demand a high dowry. If she is also beautiful, she may have many suitors. The girl must defer to her family and relatives to decide whom she should marry, although her opinion has a great deal of influence. The family looks at the suitor's credentials, such as his behavior, his family background, whether or not he is a hard worker, his ability to handle problems, and many other factors. His ability to pay the highest dowry is a strong consideration, but no self-respecting father would give his precious daughter to an unworthy man just for his dowry.

Many Dinka people have blended their traditional cultural beliefs with their Christianity. They believe that their male ancestors' spirits continue to exist after death and that each spirit must have a namesake among the living in order to maintain a position in the family. Since daughters are married off into other families, this namesake must continue through the male offspring. A male child who dies before he is initiated into the tribe is still remembered in the family and a share of the cows or wealth is reserved for him at the proper time. His next of kin, usually his brother, will be given the privilege of marrying a wife for him and naming all the children born to that marriage after him. Everyone must acknowledge the spirit of the dead brother as the father of these children. The children might address him as father when very young, but soon, they will call him their uncle, not their father. For this reason, this man will have to marry another woman in order to have a family of his own. It is a serious responsibility to maintain the continuity of the dead brother's spirit in the tribe. If not, his spirit will find no peace, and is capable of killing the other children of the family until the peace is found.

It is also custom for a brother to marry the wife of his brother who has died and left a young widow and young children. This way, the family name, identity, and dignity continues, and the children do not feel orphaned. These polygamous relationships also give a husband the opportunity to have many sons and daughters. At times, in this pastoral culture, men raid other families for control over more pasturelands. Having many sons brings more power to dominate more land, and having many daughters gives the opportunity for much wealth. For centuries, these practices have preserved the unity of the Dinka people and have trained them for community living.

18

I Take a Wife

While I was in Sudan, I wanted to revisit the area of my childhood and observe how life had changed since the civil war. Bor Town is a city in the state of Jonglei in Southern Sudan. The area of Bor runs along the Nile River and includes the Payam of Jalle. The Payam of Jalle is about thirty miles in area. The Payam is composed of three clans: the Alain, the Juet, and the Aboudit. When I was a boy, it was a fine agricultural area of villages, cultivated fields, common grazing grounds, and the bush. The children in the villages were all well clothed and clean. They had chores to do and were kept busy with games and learning. In 1983, the start of the long civil war in Sudan destroyed the city and all of of Bor Town.

I stood on a high place and gazed out over what had been productive farm and grazing land when I was a boy. I saw before me a swampy forest filled with lions, crocodiles, snakes, hippos, leopards, hyenas, and other wildlife. The swamp waters were a source for water-born diseases like bilharzia, cholera, and malaria. In the villages and farm dwellings, I saw many children who had no clothing sitting around with nothing to do. In the chaos and destruction of war, churches were destroyed, which deprived the people of any opportunities for Christian growth and the spiritual disciplines. The people were left without pastoral care and without the spiritual leadership of the church. In their fear, many of the people reverted to the practices of witchcraft and animal sacrifice. The Episcopal Church of Sudan is the largest Protestant denomination in southern Sudan, but there are not enough trained people to plant churches, so many states have no churches. Their communities are hungry for the word of God. A great need exists for churches and preachers.

As I traveled the area during my brief visit, I did my best to preach the word of God through community worship and by teaching people to pray for the sick and imprisoned. I met with the leaders of these communities, and they wanted me to come back to help in any way I could. In the once thriving area of Jalle, the people still do not have suitable houses, nor do they have adequate medical care or access to clean water. One well, which is far from the village, serves 1,500 people. The well is always crowded, day and night, and many fights occur over the limited water supply. Because water is so scarce, many people scoop drinking water from the nearby ditches, causing many diseases, especially to the young. The lack of healthcare and the unsanitary conditions broke my heart. The supply of medications I had brought with me was soon gone. People continued to approach me for medicine, so I walked twelve hours to the nearest town of Baidit in order to buy medicine for them. I did this several times, though I could never purchase enough.

Recent talks in Nairobi had stopped much of the fighting in the area, but the scars and suffering of twenty years of civil war still remained. I saw many people without legs and hands. Many children were left without parents, so they had to fend for themselves. The war claimed over two million lives and left an entire generation without the most basic education and community services. I spent time teaching some of the village children the alphabet, and they impressed me with their eagerness to learn.

While doing all of this, my family and I were continuing with marriage plans. The first step was for my mother and my uncle to inform the elders of various tribes in their area (payam) that I wanted to get married. Through the proper tribal channels, they found three suitable possibilities for me. My elders told me who the women were, and it was then my task to make arrangements to speak with these girls and to make my choice. The girls also had a choice. I made arrangements according to our customs to meet each of them to see if we would be compatible. One had a smiling face, but the smile seemed to hide what was in her heart. Another was very opposed and resistant, as though she were not yet ready for marriage. The last girl, Rebecca, spoke with a guarded heart, but her attitude was open and happy. I had first met her when we were teenagers in a refugee camp in Kenya. When I was later selected to go to America, Rebecca made her way back to South Sudan to be with her mother. So, I met Rebecca Athieng Deng again. She was very intelligent and witty, and I soon knew she was the girl I wanted. Later the two of us again met for a confidential talk, and she accepted my proposal.

After a young woman agrees to the marriage, she calls together the single young women in her circle of family and friends. The young man does the same with the single young men in his circle of family and friends. Each group discusses the marriage proposal. This gives them a chance to uncover any serious problems that might exist since their peers are always well informed about each other and members of other peer groups. After that, a representative from the young woman's group gives a report of this discussion to the bride's mother. The mother then takes this report, along with her own about the groom, to the bride's father. If the father approves, he will allow the next step, which is for the mother to call together the young married women to meet with the young man and his peers in order to learn their perspectives on the marriage. After everyone has been heard, each representative goes back to the bride's mother and gives their reports, which the mother takes back to the father. The father then permits the mother to call together the older women to meet with the young man and his peers to discern if he is a good fit. A representative from this older group of women goes to the mother with their report, which she takes it back to the father. The father checks with the younger men of his own family to hear what they have to say. Finally, after this long process, the father calls together his daughter, his wife, and any older sons to hear whether they will agree to this union. If they all agree, the father will notify his brothers and his sisters to see if they also agree, and if so, the groups of the young man and young woman are again called together for their final approval. Because of my limited time, after Rebecca accepted my proposal, the steps of the marriage were accelerated.

The time arrived for the father of the groom to call together all the elders in the community to obtain their approval. The two clans were ready to negotiate together. In order to ensure a proper setting for these negotiations, the groom's family slaughters a bull or two and has a feast. Representative members of both families come together in the spirit of trust to negotiate the details of the dowry, including the number of cows the groom must give to the family of the young woman. At this important feast, the marriage will either go forward or be stopped. My family slaughtered a bull and invited family members from both sides began to eat and discuss. They met with Rebecca's father, grandfather and their wives and agreed to their allotment of cows. After that, various other family members came according to their status and discussed the number of cows they would receive. After the families and elders were happy with the arrangement, we proceeded to the next step – the wedding celebration.

Jacob and Rebecca on their wedding day

A wedding celebration usually lasts up to eight days. It is an important time in tribal life since it gives the whole community a chance to fellowship, renew old ties, catch up on family news, and share marriage stories with the younger generation. Since only local TV and a few telephones exist, the long marriage celebrations are one of the best ways to renew family ties and catch up on the news. The celebration also gives an opportunity for the newlyweds to become acquainted with all the important members of each other's family and for their friends to wish them well.

My family slaughtered six cows in preparation for all the people coming to celebrate. Wedding celebrations provide some of the best opportunities for the young folks to perform their dancing and singing skills, and the elders join in, often surprising the young ones with what they can do. The little ones observe what will be expected of them in the future and learn the traditional dances and songs. Celebrations give the men many opportunities to discuss business, to present their views about what is happening in the community, and to discuss who is and is not to be trusted. These festivities give the women opportunities to share their cooking and sewing skills, and to discuss matters of their children. Celebrations allow the young opportunities to demonstrate their manners and to relate to a wide range of ages, from the elderly to toddlers. But best of all, the wedding celebration is an opportunity for everyone to fill up on the rich variety of food.

On the last day of the celebrations, Rebecca's uncle, her big brother, and her mother joined my mother and my uncle for the most solemn part of the ceremony. Rebecca's family members grasped her hands in theirs, while my family members took my hands in theirs. This signified that our family members stood with us and affirmed their support and their expectations for the marriage. Then our families released our hands and gave us to each other, and I took the hands of my lovely wife. The last detail was for us to decide how many girls from among Rebecca's friends would be allowed to accompany her to our home and stay with her for a week to support and provide comfort as she joined her new husband and his family. She decided to have twenty-seven girls come with her.

Before we left the ceremony, the elders presented me with an ivory cane. Throughout history, the cane or walking stick has played an important role in most cultures. They have been used as weapons, as instruments of punishment, as tools to control livestock, for ceremonial dancing, and so on. In our culture, the cane maker is a skilled craftsman who provides a valuable service to his tribe. He uses bamboo, ebony, or other exotic woods to cut a "blank." He makes sure the blank is free from any hidden flaws. After that, he shapes it on a lathe or a sander, depending on the style and purpose of the cane. If it is to become a shepherd's crook, he will slowly bend and shape it into just the right curve. If it is to be a ceremonial, walking, or hiking cane, he will make it just right for that purpose. Once shaped and sanded, the cane maker uses a clear or tinted finish, which will bring out the natural beauty of the wood. In my community, the ivory cane is given as a sign of admiration, authority, power, and respect. I felt greatly honored to receive an ivory cane from my people. I will always treasure my ivory cane.

19

Back To Texas – Alone

After our marriage, Rebecca and I spent two-and-a-half weeks with my family in Bor. Then we took a plane to Loki, Kenya. In Kenya, I took Rebecca on a very emotional trip to visit the refugee camp of Kakuma, where I had spent nine years growing up. All of my old friends were eager to see me again and to meet my wife. We had a wonderful time with much celebrating. From Kakuma, we took a bus to Nairobi, then back to Kampala. This little journey with Rebecca was such a special experience for me. Now, instead of a little "Lost Boy" walking with others in the desert with only the clothes on my back, I was a man traveling in my country with my wife. We spent twenty-nine days together with my friends and relatives.

We stayed in my cousin's house, which gave Rebecca a chance to get to know my family members better. When the time came for me to leave, we made arrangements for Rebecca to stay with my cousins. A couple of days before I was to leave, some friends accompanied us to the airport to make sure all the details were taken care of for my departure. They all waited in the waiting room while I went to check my visa. It was a good thing I did this, because I was told my visa had expired. I realized that I had been too busy to check it. The authorities said I needed to buy a new visa for one hundred fifty dollars. I went to the bank, paid for the visa, and took the receipt back to the authorities to get my new visa. Now everything was set for me to go. We all went back to Kampala. Two days later, we made the trip to the airport again. This time, I said my farewells to my family and my beloved wife, then boarded the plane for my journey back to America.

I arrived back in Houston on August 23, 2006. I moved in with some friends and began to look for another job. I did not wish to return to Midland. I had interviewed for and secured a job as a security officer at the Hotel Granduca. The lady who interviewed me knew that the "Lost Boys" had a reputation for being honest and hard workers. In that job, I learned much about American law enforcement and how to recognize clues to people's actions and motives. I learned how to handle aggression and how to deflect it. I learned even more about myself and how to present myself in public, as a person taking command or as a person being of help to others.

The president of the hotel was a kind person and a gentle leader. When I first began my job, I learned to recognize his car so that I could wave him through the gate. However, one day, he drove his other car, which I did not recognize, so I stopped him. I still did not recognize him and I politely welcomed him to Hotel Granduca and asked his last name. He gave it to me, and I looked for it on my list and told him it was not there and I could not let him pass. He smiled and asked me to call the manager or the receptionist. When I did, they told me he was the owner and I should let him pass. I quickly allowed him to pass, but he had failed to tell me that his son was following him. When the son drove up and I asked him for his name, he said he was the owner's son. I told him that the owner had not told me his son would be following, therefore, I could not let him pass until his information was verified. The son called out the window to his father who then asked me to please allow his son to pass, which I did. I was concerned that this might give me a bad reputation, but instead they laughed and said they felt safe with me at the gate.

The general manager was a very gracious lady and a source of inspiration and encouragement to all the employees of the hotel. She treated us like family. Her kind of leadership was what made working for Granduca so exciting and enjoyable. My hours were from three in the afternoon to eleven-thirty at night, and I looked forward to work every day. After five years in America, this was the first time I felt like a part of a working family.

I often brought my Bible to work to read in the lunchroom during breaks. Sometimes we had little employee gatherings or celebrations in the lunchroom, where I offered a brief reference to

God's blessings or encouragement. I was not aware that this might be offensive to some. My overseer was a little bit hostile to me because he did not like the way I so strictly followed the rules. When he heard about someone taking offense to the Bible, he saw this as an opportunity to find fault with me. He came to me and said that a new policy was set into place stating that the employees were no longer allowed to bring Bibles to work or to make any references to God at the work site.

One of the employees in housekeeping was from Sierra Leone. He claimed to be a Christian and Muslim at the same time. One day he brought his huge African Heritage Bible to work with him and left it on the security desk. The manager came in the morning and found it. I was not at work that day, and he asked around to see whose Bible it was, but no one claimed it. By this time, my fellow workers knew that the manager thought it was mine and that he was going to fire me when I came to work. They called me and warned me, so I was prepared. When I came to work, dressed in my uniform, he called me into his office and began asking me questions. He asked me why I had brought my Bible to work and broken the rules. He accused me of not taking the rules seriously, which would result in my termination. I listened patiently and told him that the Bible was not mine. He took the time to investigate this and when he discovered that I was telling the truth, he apologized and told me what a great Christian I was. He began to talk about his Catholic faith and his commitment to God. He sounded like he was trying to convince me of his Christianity, even though he had never once talked about it before or acknowledged his faith to me. At the same time, I felt that he now had allowed God to work in him, and this made me glad.

Sometime later, a Christian couple staying at the hotel asked the desk clerk if they had a Bible, because their computer was down and they wanted to look up a reference. The clerk knew that I always had my Bible with me. She called me on the job and asked if I could bring my Bible to the desk. She was not aware of the change in policy. I told her that I had my Bible in the car but was not allowed to bring it into the workplace. I was sorry, but she said that was okay.

After working at Granduca for six months or so, I had saved enough money to get my U.S. citizenship. I filled out the paperwork and started the process. I sent the papers to Immigration and waited for further instructions. They sent me the appointment letter for my fingerprints. After that, they gave me a book to study for my citizenship test. I received a letter in the mail with my interview date. The interview took place in a huge, impressive hall, where a very tough-sounding judge called my name. When I stood, he yelled for me to go across the street and get my passport photos taken. I asked what happened to the photographs I had sent, and he sternly told me to do what he said. He was such a scary judge. I went across the street, got my photographs, and returned to my place in the hall. Soon, he came back out of his office and called my name. This time, I answered, "Yes sir." He took me into the office where I answered the questions, took the oath of allegiance, and wrote a sentence about my citizenship. Then he shook my hand and congratulated me on passing my test of citizenship. He told me that I needed to go to the ceremony that was to take place at the Great Hall on January 24, 2007.

Before that day arrived, I received a phone call telling me that I was selected to be specially honored because of the struggles I had endured. When I arrived for the ceremony, three very long lines of people were outside the building. I was not sure where to go, so I walked up to the door, but did not go in because there was also a long line of people inside. I went back outside to the end of one of the long lines. A lady official saw my name tag and approached me, telling me to follow her. Everyone watched as she took me past the line and into the building. Inside, they took my green card, punched a hole in it, and told me I did not need it any more because I was a citizen. That was exciting to hear. Then, they sat me to the side of the room in a huge empty section all by myself.

The lady who had brought me inside was an INS judge, and she brought some other people by and asked if I knew them. When I said no, she sent them away. They told me this section was reserved for only my friends and myself. I saw some of my "Lost Boys" friends and called out for them to join me. I asked the official why I was chosen, and she said because I deserved recognition after my many struggles to get to this point. Then, another official came to me, gave me a paper, and asked me to write a letter to the United States about some of my struggles. When I finished the letter, he took it to the lady judge who was presiding, and she read it to the people during the ceremony. After she read it she thanked me and said she was happy that God had brought us to the United States. She welcomed all of us to our new life as citizens. We were told to wait after the ceremony for someone to bring our citizenship papers to sign. The ceremony was full of great encouragement for me. I felt their care for me and for everyone else who became citizens. This was one of the biggest moments in my life in America. After experiencing many moments of being dishonored and rejected, I will never forget how good it felt to be honored and respected in America.

When I went back to work, I felt that I belonged. One afternoon, as I was making my security rounds, one of the guests was walking around the parking lot admiring the front of the hotel. That day in mid-August was very hot, but he stopped to talk with me. He inquired about me, and I told him I was Sudanese. He said he was a supporter of an organization that helped Sudanese in Tennessee. He asked me if I was a Christian. When I said I was, we began to discuss the Bible. We had a wonderful conversation, and I continue to email Terry, while he and his wife offer their prayers for my work. Their support has also made an immense impression on me.

20
Rebecca's Immigration Saga

I had started the process of Rebecca's immigration to the United States. I arranged for her to move from Uganda to Nakuru, Kenya to be with my sister and cousin. This way, she would be close to the immigration offices, since I knew she would need to make many visits there. I flew out to visit and encourage her as she started this difficult process. This time, I was traveling as a U.S. citizen. It was a great deal easier to pass through various immigration points, especially in Kenya, because they did not allow green card holders from the U.S. to enter the country. When I landed in Nairobi, they were having one of their many political crises, which was frightening. Rebecca was waiting for me at the airport and told me about the situation.

Due to the political uprising, all of the roads were blocked to prevent the two opposing groups from coming into contact. After two days in Nairobi, I was able to find a cab driver who said he knew how to get us to Nakuru safely, but it would cost me a lot of money. I paid him the money, and he got us to Nakuru. The roads were also blocked there, but we were able to get to the apartment that Rebecca had rented for us. While there, I received a call from my bishop from the Episcopal Church in Sudan, who was visiting the Sudanese church in Nairobi. He informed me that the church deaconry had recommended me for ordination as a deacon. He wanted me to meet with him and discuss the process. I told him I was in the middle of doing many legal tasks and was not sure a meeting would be convenient. He asked for me to pray and speak with my wife, and he gave me three days to make a decision. I discussed the situation with Rebecca, and we decided I should go ahead with the meeting. In spite of the unsettled conditions around us, we managed to go back to Nairobi, where I received my ordination on February 3, 2008. After that, we went back to Nakuru to say goodbye to our relatives. Then Rebecca and I returned to Nairobi for my flight home. I arrived back in the United States on February 26, 2008. I returned to my job and to the apartment where my roommate welcomed me. Then I checked in with my lawyer to make sure he was continuing with the immigration process for my wife.

The days passed quickly. I enjoyed going to church, socializing and I felt comfortable hanging out with Americans as well as with my native friends. Every weekend I checked in with Rebecca. One month after I had returned, when I called Rebecca, she had some very exciting news. She told me she was pregnant. I was really excited, but I was not yet ready to make the news public. In my culture, a marriage without a baby brings stress into the relationship. It signifies that God may not be with you, or that one of you has a problem. A baby cements the relationship and binds the couple together with a love that would not happen otherwise. The news was of such a magnitude that I was reluctant to share it with my friends right away. I first wanted to be sure all was well. After three months, I shared our pregnancy with my dearest friends, Tim, Jason, Chris, and their wives.

One night, during the first week of August, 2008, I got home from work at eleven-thirty at night, took a shower, and sat down to watch some news, as I usually did before I went to bed. When I lay down, I could not sleep, but a vision came to me. I saw my bishop, another bishop and a number of pastors surrounding me. I was wearing my deacon cloth on my side, as deacons do. My bishop came over and moved the cloth to the front, telling me that I was now ordained as a pastor. I turned around to speak to them, but they had all disappeared. After this vision, I could not sleep, so I watched TV. I knocked on my roommate's door to talk to him, but he did not answer. After awhile, I went back to bed, but I still could not sleep. I prayed to God and told him I did not know what the vision meant, but that I was willing to do whatever he was asking me to do.

That afternoon when I went to work, I shared my vision with my friend, Dut Dau, a "Lost Boy" with whom I worked. He asked me how such a thing could happen, since the bishop was in Africa and I was here. He suggested I should not share the vision because if it did not happen, I would appear to be a liar. I dropped my head because I felt he suspected me of lying. Then, I confidently told him that this was not a lie. I did not know how or where it was going to happen, but it definitely was going to happen in August.

In the second week of August, I received a call from my lawyer saying that my wife was scheduled for an interview in Kenya on September 2. He said that I needed to be there for the interview. I told him I would go. He advised that when I bought my ticket, I should also buy a ticket for Rebecca, so she could come back with me. I assured him that this would be foolish because the immigration process is very complicated and would not be finished in such a short time. He insisted that I needed to get her a ticket. I told him I would share this with my friends at church and see what they had to say. I presented the situation to my friends Tim and Summer, Jason and Erin, and Chris and Jamie. They gathered around me and told me that the lawyer's advice should be followed. They offered to buy Rebecca's ticket. I told them it would be a waste of money because I knew that she would not be able to return with me. Then, I told them that even though I was being called back to Africa for the interview at this specific time, I felt God had another reason besides the interview to call me back to Africa. They eagerly asked me what I was talking about, but I was not ready to share my vision with them. Instead, I told them Rebecca could not possibly get through the immigration process in time to return with me, but since they insisted on buying her ticket, I let them.

I got all my immigration paperwork and my shots completed before the end of August. On August 27th, I called my cousin who lives in Kenya, Pastor Antipas Mayen Biar, to advise him I was coming and would arrive on August 29 at 8:00 p.m. Kenya time. He expressed surprise at hearing from me, and told me he and my bishop had just been talking about me. The Bishop had told Antipas that if I happened to be coming anytime soon, he would arrange for me to be ordained as a pastor! I told Antipas that this is what I expected to happen. Antipas sounded a bit incredulous, and told me that it could not happen because the Bishop was leaving for Australia on the day that I was to arrive. I told him that if God wanted me to be ordained in August, God would either detain the Bishop or find another way. Antipas thought my prediction was very tenuous, but said he would make preparations for me.

I had sent money ahead to Antipas so he could arrange for a taxi to bring Rebecca and two friends to the airport to meet me. In the taxi on our way to Rebecca's apartment, Antipas called Rebecca on her cell phone and asked if he could speak with me. She handed me the phone. Antipas told me that he had told the Bishop I was coming, and the Bishop said that he wanted to meet with me on August 30 to arrange for my ordination on the thirty-first. I asked why the Bishop was not on his way to Australia, and Antipas said it was because his visa would not be ready for another few days. And so, I received my ordination in August according to the vision God had given me.

On Monday, the first of September, I went with Rebecca to the hospital to get the medical records for a chest x-ray and a shot she had received. The doctor said these papers were required for immigration. Rebecca informed me that she already had the x-ray and shot done in Nakuru months before and had brought those papers with her to the doctor in Nairobi so she could get her immigration papers. Unfortunately, the secretary in the Nairobi office kept putting Rebecca off. They told her to come back for it many times, but they never gave it to her. This time, I went with her, and we arrived at the hospital at six in the morning. Just as before, they told us to wait in the waiting room. While we were waiting, we watched as, one by one, they told everyone else in the waiting room to go in. By noon, I was exasperated, so I went to the nurse and asked to speak with the doctor. She told me to wait and she would tell him that I wanted to speak with him. I watched her as she crossed to the back of the office and returned without seeing the doctor. She told me she spoke with him and he would see me soon. I knew she did not see him, but my patience was still intact, so I sat for another hour. Then, I asked the secretary if she would please tell the doctor that I would like to see him. She said she would. I observed closely as she went into the back office and came out again. I was pretty sure she had not done what I asked. She told me to sit and wait and he would see me soon. So, this time I stood outside his office and waited until I saw his patient leave.

Then I quickly slipped into the office. The nurses and the secretary ran into the office after me saying I could not do this. The doctor told them to be quiet and let me talk. I asked them if it was a sin for me to talk to the doctor, since they had not been able to get him to speak to me. I explained to him that my wife had been coming to this office for over a month trying to get her records for immigration and that we had been waiting since six in the morning today. I explained that our interview was scheduled for the next morning with the immigration office and that we needed her records. The doctor said he would write a letter for me to take to immigration. So, we went out to wait. Soon, the nurse brought out the letter along with the chest x-ray.

The next morning, when we took the letter and the papers to the immigration office, the officials said that the x-ray was valid, but the shot record was not. It was a photocopy and they needed the original. I returned to the doctor, and he told me that since Rebecca's examination was in Nakuru, she would need to go there to get the original record. So, we both went to the bus station and took a bus to Nakuru, over two hours away. By this time, Rebecca was very tired, since she was pregnant. We arrived in Nakuru at night. Just about the time we arrived at the doctor's office, the lights went out in the whole area. The doctor told us he was sorry, but we had to come back in the morning so he could see to read the papers. We went to our apartment and got some sleep. We got up early the next morning to go back to the hospital. This time, we got the records and hurried back to Nairobi. I called the immigration office and made an appointment for October 6, 2008. I could not stay that long because I had to report back to work in the United States by September 11. So, I said my goodbyes to Rebecca and returned home.

21

From Chaos To Completion

When Rebecca went to her appointment in October, she was very pregnant. She sat waiting at the immigration office for eight hours. At four in the afternoon, the security guard, who had seen her there all day, asked the secretary and nurse why they would make a pregnant woman wait in the office over eight hours. They apologized to Rebecca and said that the computers were down. They told her to come back the next day. By this time, Rebecca was drained of energy, and she decided she did not want to continue the immigration process at all. I sympathized with her over the phone and said I understood, but I asked her if she would please try one more time, and then, if they did not give her the papers, I would stop the process. She agreed. She went back the next day. This time, they gave the papers to her. However, since she was pregnant, she would have to have a DNA test for the baby after it was born to prove that I was the father. So, we agreed that she should return to Nakuru and have the baby first, then complete the process. She returned, and our son Biar was born in Nakuru on October 20, 2008. We started the immigration process again, but this time with our son.

I did not realize the amount of work it would take to get my son to the United States. First, I went to a lawyer who was recommended by my church. We discussed the situation for about an hour-and-a-half in his office. He was kind and very helpful; however, he could do nothing until I had a birth certificate. He then gave me the necessary requirements needed to obtain the birth certificate. I called Rebecca, who was in Kenya, and asked her to get Biar's birth certificate and email it to me. It took Rebecca three months to go through the process of getting the birth certificate, but she was finally able to email it to me. With the birth certificate in hand, I again went to the lawyer. The lawyer asked me a list of personal questions, which I did not feel were relevant to the situation, that consumed a lot of expensive time. So, I decided to continue the process on my own. I went online to the immigration website and filled out all the forms needed to report a childbirth abroad. Next, I filled out the Social Security and parental affidavit paperwork. Then, I filled out a passport application for Biar. I had to photocopy all my documents for naturalization, my Social Security card, passport, visa, state ID, and all of Biar's paperwork to be notarized. Finally, I sent all the paperwork to my wife in Kenya.

Rebecca received the paperwork and took it to the American Embassy. The embassy said that the paperwork was not properly filled out, and told Rebecca to go away. She stood her ground and asked them to explain to her where the paperwork was incorrect so that she could pass that information on to me. They insisted that she leave, so she did. She called me that evening, and I told her to go back and get the precise information I needed. The next day she returned to the embassy at 8:00 a.m. and waited until 4:00 p.m. before they spoke to her. They again turned her away. On the third day, at her insistence, they finally, with much disdain and disrespect, gave her what she needed. When she got the necessary paperwork, she sent it to me by FedEx. When I looked over the paperwork, I realized what they wanted was the very same paperwork I had sent. I did this four times over the next four weeks while poor Rebecca resubmitted them. Each time, they refused to accept them.

By this time, Rebecca had spent a great deal of time and energy traveling by bus to the embassy with our newborn son. She was getting tired and discouraged. To make matters worse, Biar was not feeling well. She called and said that the stress of getting the papers was not worth making the baby sick. She wanted to quit. I was very frustrated that the embassy was not more cooperative, and I pleaded with her to try one more time. She agreed, and we went through the process one more time. I thank God that all the paperwork was finally accepted.

After all the fees were paid, the next step was for us to have a record of our DNA. For that I had to fill out another whole set of paperwork and send it and a hefty fee to the Center for DNA in the United States. In order for Rebecca to get her and Biar's DNA, I had to have the paperwork sent to the embassy in Kenya as well. Rebecca went to the embassy, and they acknowledged they had received the paperwork and would forward it to their doctor. They sent her to the doctor's office, where they told her they did not have the paperwork. So Rebecca, with little Biar, returned to the embassy and they again sent her back to the doctor. She did this three times and finally got the DNA papers, which, surprisingly, finally managed to arrive at the doctor's. They then sent all the processed DNA reports back to Kenya.

By this time I had learned a thing or two about the immigration process, so I had tracked the DNA papers and saw online that they had arrived back at the embassy in Kenya. However, when Rebecca went for them, she was told they were not there. But the second time she went back, they were there! The embassy told her they would begin the process for Biar's passport and she was to return in two weeks. When she did, miraculously, she got the passport the first time. But, on that day, they also took her passport to give her a visa and told her to return again in two weeks. She was leery of doing this, but she did it. Again, miraculously, they gave her a visa as promised. I bought them a ticket on KLM airlines to come to America, and we rejoiced. Rebecca packed all her things, gave up her apartment, and went to the airport in Kenya. At the airport, she was told that because Biar had American citizenship through his father, he could board the plane, but she could not because she did not have a transient visa. They told her she would have to get one to board the plane with him. This seemed to be an impossible situation! She went to the home of some friends and called me. At this point I was out of money, and Rebecca was running out of patience and energy. She told me that she was not willing to come to America. After being treated so badly by the American Embassy, she was afraid of how she might be treated in America. I kept encouraging her that no matter how hard the struggles, life would go well for her here.

I quickly appealed to my friends in my Sunday school class, and they decided to help me. They were able to get a ticket on a Turkish airline the next day, so Rebecca had to rush back to the airport. At 3:00 a.m., she and baby Biar finally boarded the plane, and they were on their way. She left Kenya on March 11 and arrived in New York on March 12 at 5:00 p.m. My brave wife, wearied by the endless process, the disrespect, and speaking no English, traveled with a four-month old baby from Nairobi to New York! When I look back on that time, I cannot believe how she endured the whole situation. I give all the praise and glory to God for working out the problems and for sustaining my dear wife through that frustrating journey.

When Rebecca and Biar arrived in America, some of my "Lost Boy" friends who lived in New York met them and invited them to stay until she could board the flight to Houston the next day. At long last, she arrived in Houston on Friday, March 13 at 10:00 p.m. I was so excited to finally be with my Rebecca again and to see my son. It was a thrilling moment, but we were both so exhausted that we were in no mood to celebrate. I took her to my apartment, which I shared with my cousin, and we all went to bed to sleep. That first night in Houston, little Biar was not feeling well and he woke up crying every twenty minutes. My cousin came back from work at five in the morning to two exhausted parents and a crying baby. He looked at me carrying the crying baby while I was trying to allow Rebecca to get some sleep, and he commented, "So this is what family life is like?"

That Sunday, my church class wanted to give Rebecca a welcome celebration. They had a wonderful, warm welcome for her and presented her with little gifts of toys, diapers, and baby clothes for Biar. This made her feel much better about the move.

After the move, Biar was not gaining weight, and we became concerned. Rebecca was worried because he was not nursing well. I had no idea what to do or how to go about getting medical attention for him. I found a pediatrician through a friend. The doctor asked if I had insurance and I said no, but I was willing to pay. So the doctor saw Biar and put him through a series of tests. We saw the doctor three times, but he found nothing that would cause his weight loss. He then referred us to the Texas Children's Hospital for more tests. I was quite frustrated and the doctor could sense that was I ready to refuse any more tests for my son. He then told me that he would send an ambulance to get Biar if I did not take him, so I took him to the hospital.

The doctor directed us to take him to the emergency room. A friend of mine went along to help Rebecca with the language and be with her when I had to leave for work. After all of the months of problems in coming to the United States, she was now again enduring the anxiety of a hospital. We arrived at the emergency room at 10:00 a.m. I had to leave for work at 1:00 p.m.. By 6:00 p.m., when my friend had to leave, Biar still had not been admitted. Rebecca continued to wait with him until finally, at midnight, he was admitted. I arrived at 12:30 a.m. with some food, but Rebecca was too stressed and exhausted to eat. I realized that she was not yet adjusted to the food here, so I left the room and walked about outside, looking for some kind of grocery that would sell something fresh she would eat. I finally found a Subway and took her a sandwich. She nibbled at it even though she was not actually hungry. The tests found nothing wrong with Biar, but the TB skin test was positive so they ran some tests on his lungs. His lungs were fine so after three days he was discharged. They recommended we administer some TB medicine just to cover all bases, which we did.

22

Moving To Pennsylvania

About that time, I had been in touch with Bill Butler, who said he wanted us to move to Lancaster, Pennsylvania, since he was the co-signer of Rebecca's immigration papers. He wanted to be sure that we would be close to his family. I was not sure that was where God wanted us, so I told him that I would first apply to Lancaster Bible College. If they accepted me, then I would come. The college did accept me, and we made plans to go to Lancaster.

I knew that I would have to work, so helping us get settled would fall on Bill. He told us not to worry, but to come on to Lancaster. Then the generous man flew to Houston, rented a truck, and helped us load it. Rebecca and Biar had arrangements to fly, so they would be there waiting for us. Bill and I packed the truck and started for Lancaster. For me, it was a very exciting trip. I had never traveled across country by car, and I thoroughly enjoyed watching the scenery fly by. Bill had forgotten to register me as one of the drivers, so he had to do all the driving. But he gave me the map to read, which I was happy to do. We made the 1,500-mile trip in two days. The Butlers offered us the use of their home until I could find an apartment. The church had an empty apartment on its property, which we were able to rent. Rebecca was pregnant again, and the Butlers also helped her get to the hospital for her appointments.

The people at Lancaster Bible College were wonderful to me during my registration. They guided me through the admission process and helped me choose the needed courses. Sometimes, friends helped with transportation to and from college and work until I could get a car.

Meanwhile, Rebecca set up house and learned about city living in Lancaster. She had some tremendous adjustments to make. In South Sudan, she would have been a part of a community, surrounded by relatives and friends to help with the cooking, the chores, and as well the care of Biar. She was pretty much alone inside a little apartment all day, pregnant and caring for a toddler. I was unable to give her much help since I needed to spend so much time on my studies and had to be at school or at work.

Hospital appointments were very frustrating for Rebecca, particularly with the difficulty of language. As you can imagine, no hospital in Lancaster had anyone who could speak Dinka. But hospitals have an international phone service that allows them to make contact with a number of translators around the States. The hospital used this service when Rebecca had appointments. One day at the hospital, I was in the waiting room while she was in the examining room with the translator on the phone. She was having a problem with the translator and getting very frustrated. The problem was that the translator was speaking a different dialect of the Dinka language, so they used me instead.

On February 23, 2010, Rebecca went to the hospital with her friend for a routine checkup while I was at school. She began having contractions during her appointment, and the hospital said she had to stay. I went to the hospital to help her get admitted, while one of the church members took care of Biar. Rebecca was concerned because she had heard from some of our Sudanese friends in America that doctors are sometimes quick to perform Cesarean sections and she wanted a natural delivery. They also wanted to give her pain medication, which she did not want. We signed papers stating that, because we were afraid they might give her something without our knowledge. In her village, Rebecca observed many women who were in labor for several days before they delivered, and it did not seem to harm the mothers or the babies. She spent three days in the hospital before delivering our little girl, who weighed five pounds, nine ounces. She was beautiful. When our daughter, Angeth Guot, arrived, it was a happy time because my family was surrounded by caring hearts.

After Angeth was born, Rebecca began to feel more settled, but she still had many adjustments to make. She was not acquainted with many of the American foods and didn't know the names of the foods she recognized. She did not know very much English, so she could not ask anyone, which made grocery shopping very difficult. At home, Rebecca had a collection of embroidered cloths from our village which she hung over curtain rods and the backs of chairs. Coming home each day, I was encouraged because our living room was decorated with welcoming, traditional Dinka designs. Even during the stressful processes of shopping, attending doctor's appointments, and cooking meals, she was patient and supportive. I remember coming home one evening so angry about something that disappointed me, and she lovingly reassured me that I needed to leave this anger in God's hands rather than bring it home and go to bed with it. Another night, I was supposed to do the grocery shopping, but I was so busy that I forgot. When I got home, she did not get angry with me, but told me in a gentle way that she understood. She always had supper ready, and did everything she could to make the family and me comfortable. I hear many men bragging about their wives because they are look sexy, or are good cooks or very smart, but none of this is as valuable as a loving heart and a gentle spirit. My wife reminds me of the beauty of God's plan for both the woman and the man in marriage. She inspires me to do everything I need to do to support her. I am sure there were many times when Rebecca became discouraged and wanted to leave, but she never said so to me. Rather than discourage me, she was always hopeful for the future of our family. She was always ready to do what was needed for me to continue to work and finish school. I was so grateful for her patience and her kindness, especially because I was back on the hunt for a job in Pennsylvania.

After many hours of standing in line and taking tests, I got a job at a company named R.R. Donnelly. They have a policy that everyone must be available to work all shifts, so I started working all kinds of hours. After discovering I was a good worker, my supervisor worked out a suitable schedule for me so that I could continue with my education. I was working, I was supporting my family, and I was continuing my studies.

23
Higher Education

My classes at Lancaster Bible College took place on Tuesday evenings. I was expecting the professors to simply lecture to us, but to my surprise they wanted to know who we were. One of my first courses was on C.S. Lewis. We read *The Lion, The Witch, and the Wardrobe*, a story which seemed very strange to me at first, as I had never read an allegory before. We also read *The Screwtape Letters*, which gave me insights into the way Satan works and how we can mount our defenses against him. I had never written a class paper before. My professor wrote many notes on my first attempts, which guided me in the ways he wanted me to think and reflect on the readings. I began to understand the lessons he wanted me to take from the stories. I took an ethics class from the same professor and made the same grade in that class as I had in the other. When I saw this, I asked him whether he even read my papers, or if he just used the same grade as my other papers. He laughed and assured me that he had seen the papers and the grade was adequate. He was very kind and gave me extra time to compensate for my language difficulties.

Every class was a great adventure. I leaned much from my Bible history course and from the history of the Western world course. I read about the influences that shaped the great churches in the West, something which I knew nothing about. I had to learn about the Roman Empire, the European city-states, and the various struggles between the governing forces and the church. Countries like Italy, Greece, Spain, and Switzerland, which are familiar to Western college students, were all new to me. I did not know where these countries were, their relationships to one another, or which city belonged to which country. I was learning

Western geography as well as Western history! But I studied hard.

The dean of the degree completion program at the college taught a group dynamics class that nearly blasted my mind! (our common term for this is "blew my mind" but I like "blasted" better). His class made me face not only the tremendous diversity God designed into his world, but, most exciting of all, how God can use this diversity to draw people together rather than divide them! That was a concept I had never considered. In my mind, diversity had been the line that divided us, and those divisions needed to be protected in order for us to maintain our integrity against the "other side." This was deeply ingrained in my thinking. I hadn't realized that such a mindset could be hostile to God! I never imagined that diversity not only came from God, but was also to be considered a gift to be preserved! In that class, we learned how to use this diversity to bring people together rather than divide them and how to talk through these diverse issues. I learned to be careful to maintain people's dignity in light of disagreements. I learned the vital role that small groups can play in bringing people together and introducing truth and light into their thinking. I learned that the Christian Church can use the Bible and the power of Jesus to find common ground on which all can stand. The professor encouraged us to look for strategies to restore people and to use group dynamics to minister to them.

Jesus did not give a complete set of specific laws and rituals like the ones in the Old Testament, and he even departed from some of these. In the Beatitudes, he taught from the standpoint of change, saying, "you have heard it said... But I tell you." Jesus puts the burden of responsibility for our actions on our renewed hearts, rather than upon the law, allowing the Holy Spirit to guide us. The Holy Spirit will not negate the law, but will lead us into a compassionate response. These lessons will be invaluable for me as I try to bring hope and restoration to my people in Sudan.

The class I took on psychology challenged my thinking even more. Psychology taught me how the physical parts of our brains process knowledge and give us understanding. It taught me that the very physiological equipment through which we learn about God was precisely designed by God to learn about him! This blend of the physical and spiritual gave me a larger view of God's inescapable hand working in his world.

The psychology class showed me what a worldview is and put me in touch with my own. Belief systems that form our worldviews are built through our families, cultures, and environments. I became aware that our worldviews can, and almost always do, contain many erroneous concepts, which can lead us far astray. Knowing what lies behind our worldview is important.

A class called "Christ and Culture" helped me understand the basic principles of life that apply to all human cultures. I began to see how the teachings of Jesus fit into all cultures and bring light into the hearts of all peoples. This light enables people to change cultures for the benefit of the people, rather than for corruption. The professor showed us how the Bible applied in all areas of life, from political action to marriage relationships.

The same professor taught a wonderful class on the book of Romans where I began to see more clearly how God used Jesus in the plan of salvation. This class gave me meaningful insights into how every area of our lives is touched by how we think and process information. It taught me that the Church plays a vital role of representing God in all of these areas.

Not only did my classes help me recognize the need for God's guidance in the affairs of the world, they gave me a deep appreciation for the sacrifice and deep knowledge of those who wrote and preserved our Bible. The Bible has always been precious to my people and myself, but as the Ethiopian asked Philip, "How can I understand unless someone explains it to me?" (Acts 8:31, NIV). Lancaster Bible College had done for me what Philip did for the Ethiopian.

The Dean's assistant kept track of the students and helped them with any problems they were having. She dealt with the students' schedules and made sure they took the classes they needed, while guiding them through mounds of paper work. She was very patient, always had a smile, and expressed interest in us on a personal level. This was very important to me. She would email me often to alert me to changes in the schedule or events happening on campus. She spent a lot of time making sure we all had our courses in order, were able to get our homework in on time, and were able to attend classes. I once told her that I did not want a course that was on my schedule because I did not feel it would be useful for me. When she saw that she could not convince me to take it, she found a substitute course for me.

Meanwhile, Rebecca was home caring for the two little ones while I worked all week and attended school on Tuesday nights. I found an ESL program for her, and she began to attend. By this time, Biar was going to the pre-school program at the church, so he began to interact with other children and learn English. Rebecca quickly learned the basics, but life was not easy for her, especially in the cold winter. She spent much time alone with the children, since none of our Sudanese friends lived close to us.

24

Learning to Work in America

I learned about other aspects of life in America through my work at R. R. Donnelley, a huge company that puts together pamphlets, telephone books, and magazines. According to my work description, I was a materials handler. I checked the stock, aligned machines to fit the stock, ensured the papers for the machine were in the correct order, and loaded the machine. We worked with high tech machines that needed to be fed paper in a very precise order. When the machine misfired or the paper messed up, corrections had to be made. The faster the problem was fixed, the more efficiently the work could be completed.

I tend to be quite competent with machines, and when I understand the problem, I can fix the machine rather quickly. However, I was not really sure how to respond to the attitudes and language of some of my co-workers. When I came to work, I would give them a hearty greeting and a big smile, because this is how we greet one another in our culture. Many of them ignored me. Others gave me weird looks, and others even sneered with disapproval. One fellow asked why I always was smiling. When I told him that I was happy to have a job and enjoyed coming to work every day, he called me crazy. I felt rejected and went to my supervisor and explained the problem. He laughed and told me they did not mean any harm, they were just not used to my ways. So I asked him to help me understand their customs, so I could work with them better. He told me that it was not customary to greet your co-workers with a smile, since this was not a party. I asked if it is better if I do not greet them at all, and he laughed again and told me that it would be okay to greet them. Many of my people skills had been developed in church, and I saw that in

123

this regard, the workplace might be different than the church. Another custom in my culture is for people to dress up in public, and I liked wearing a suit to the work place. That also drew many comments. One co-worker asked whether I was dressing for church, or for work. After that, I dressed down a bit so that I was not a distraction.

Another time, my co-worker told me I should only work hard when the supervisor was around. At my look of surprise, he explained that a person works hard when the supervisor is watching so that he gets a good reputation, but when the supervisor is not around, the worker takes it easy. I asked what the point of that was. He declared there was no reason to kill myself working. He told me that the longer one worked there, the more he would be able to get away with, and I needed to learn these skills.

My co-workers had learned to work together and pretend to help a person reload, when they were really only getting together to chat. I asked them why I should learn that kind of work when I was only interested in getting the job done. They told me that it would be in my best interest to do it their way because, if I did not, they would see to it that my station would not operate well. They could do this by mis-feeding my station, allowing the paper to spill out when it was full, or other devious actions. I told them that my habit was to give my work everything I could for the benefit of the company, and I would continue to do that. I said that hard work is actually more beneficial. Getting the work out quickly and efficiently was in our best interests because it made the company prosper, which in turn improved our chances of more work and better pay. They replied that they were just trying to clue me in because they cared about me. I think my logic was more than they could handle, because after that they just shook their heads and left me alone.

My co-workers came from various backgrounds. Some seemed to be opposed to working with a big, black person, and they expressed their opposition very colorfully. Some of their words I had never heard before, and I often had to ask my supervisor what they meant. Many times, he was shocked and embarrassed as he defined the words for me, but then he would laugh. He helped me understand where my co-workers were coming from. I gradually began to catch on to the system. I learned that when a person registers a complaint, it is noted, but if he registers another, he becomes known as a troublemaker and he, rather than the offender, attracts negative attention from the supervisors. My supervisor urged me to have patience for the situations in which most of these people lived, and he encouraged me to work with them rather than in opposition to them. I did not ever report anyone, because I learned that they would support one another against me if I did. I talked with my supervisor a lot and learned how to work out problems. I learned much from all of the supervisors and workers who really cared about the company and worked very hard to keep it running smoothly.

One time, a woman I was working with used the term "dark chocolate" to describe me. I asked her if my color meant she could not treat me as a human being. She began to think about my question, and to her credit, she began to explore her attitudes more deeply. She told me her dad did not like blacks because she had hooked up with one. To him, this was like joining a race of lazy people who had no skills to work or make an honest living with. So I asked her if I fit that description. We managed to work together. More than once, a person who was hostile to me later apologized and became my friend.

My work at Donnelley showed me how to deal with everyday problems encountered in the workplace. I got a glimpse of life in the working-class cultural setting. I learned that all walks of life have their ugly sides, and that a person who is looking just at the ugly side of life can find it in the workplace, along with plenty of good, honest, hard workers. I am grateful for the lessons I learned from the people and the supervisors at R. R. Donnelley. I am also grateful for my supervisor's thoughtful scheduling that enabled me to continue my schooling and plan for my next trip to South Sudan.

25
A Visit to South Sudan

Pastor Kent and I were planning a trip to South Sudan. Several friends offered Kent gifts of money for our trip, and one of his friends gave him frequent flyer miles on two different airlines as well. Kent was able to get us both on the same flights to and from Kampala ,and our seats were right next to each other. On May 25, 2011, we left New York for Kampala, Uganda. My brother John Lual Nyok, Pastor Abel, and Mabior Buol met us at Kampala, where we rested for the night. The next day, we traveled by bus to Nimule, Sudan. There, my family had arranged a car and hotel room for us to use during our visit. After we had a shower and a short rest, some of my friends and family members visited. Then, all of us went to my village where my mother lives. I hadn't seen her since 2006. My sister, who had helped my mother while rearing her own three children, had died in 2009. Now, my mother was raising the children. Another one of my sisters and her two children were also living with my mother, since she was elderly and needed their help.

Jacob and some family members, on his last visit to South Sudan.
From left, Jacob's uncle, Jook Ayiei Biar, Jacob, his sister,
Angeth Guor Ayiei, and his mother.

Our family and clan held a big celebration to thank Kent and the First United Methodist Church of Lancaster for their steady support of John Lual through his high school and university education. The community church, St. Stephen's Episcopal Church, and the entire community wanted to express their thanks and give honor to Pastor Kent. They slaughtered a steer, and we all had a great feast together. Before we left the U.S.A, they had asked me to preach for them on Sunday, which I did. Many people came to hear me preach. What a wonderful time!

We then took a 130-mile bus trip north to Juba, the temporary capital of the then-emerging nation of South Sudan. My cousin Biar Thuch Ayiei, who greatly helped us on our trip, accompanied us to make sure we were protected on our way Juba. In Juba, several pastor friends came from Bor Town to meet with me. In addition, I met with several government officials. Kent told me that wherever we went, everybody seemed to know me!

After a few days in Juba, we boarded a bus to return to Kampala. The bus stopped for an hour in the Nimule district, where several family and village members came to greet us. We all stood alongside the dirt road hugging and talking. I knew then that I would probably not see my mother or family again until I finished seminary and returned to South Sudan to do mission work.

Before concluding our trip, Kent and I returned to Kampala to try and meet with the Methodist bishop. The Methodists have only one bishop in East Africa, the Bishop of the East Africa Annual Conference of The United Methodist Church, who is based in Kampala. The day happened to be a Ugandan holiday and the Conference office was closed, but we were able to get hold of his secretary and we did meet with him.

26
The Value of Education

On December 16, 2011, I received my degree from Lancaster Bible College and Graduate School. As I walked across the campus carrying my gown, cap, and tassel, a lady who had previously discussed the importance of education with me approached with a big smile and congratulated me. She said Americans have always recognized the importance of education, because it helps people work together and achieve great things. I realized that education is generally assumed to be used for good, but it also can be used in detrimental and dangerous ways.

If we look carefully at the roots of American education, we can see ways in which it differs from education in many other countries. We can see the influence of Christianity in the formation of the government, and the public education system was founded with a similar influence. Educational programs were formed around biblical principles. The free public education initiated in America was for the express purpose of training godly citizens. The early school curriculum included prayers and Bible lessons. As late as 1940, the National Education Association printed the Lord's Prayer on the back of leaflets that were given to the students to take home. Thus, American education was undergirded with the Christian ethics that taught young citizens to respect one another rather than tear down one another. They were taught to be listeners and to love one another rather than hating those different from themselves. They were taught to engage with strangers, help the poor, and feed the hungry. They were taught to work together toward the common good, even if they had disagreements. No country is perfect, but real leaders are those who can inspire these ideals that form a basis for real peace and success.

In South Sudan, I see another way of life operating. So many different languages and so much warfare and devastation have divided South Sudan. The people have lost all trust in one another. They have developed a philosophy of pure survival. Everyone wants to be first, because they believe the first is entitled to take the best. No one is to be trusted, except your closest friend. In such a society, people cannot work together. Brother and sister turn against one another. In such a society, people will blame each other rather than cooperate. The community divides against itself, and no form of government is able to instill peace and trust among them. The people with this mindset scorn those who fall and oppose those who succeed. Such a mindset is often the product of constant war and social disruption and leads to a totalitarian government. With such a mindset, how can people work together? The truth is, they cannot.

In South Sudan, I have witnessed great minds wasted due to a lack of education. My people have a great desire to be educated, and I feel we must include the knowledge of God in our education. Even in America, I have noticed a general atmosphere of degradation as God is being pulled out of schools, the government, and many homes. If Americans are suffering the consequences of rejecting God, we in South Sudan will also suffer if we do not allow God to work in us. South Sudanese citizens, whether in our own country or in the diaspora, need to learn what the early American citizens learned, that God's ways are higher than human ways.

We must learn that although our enemies attempted to destroy us, God rescued us, and we must give him the glory. To continue to blame our enemies for our present problems is to continue the cycle of failure. To continue to blame our enemies is to continue to fear them, which gives them power over us. The cycle of blame prevents us from forgiving not only our enemies but also ourselves for our own shortcomings. If we are jealous of one another, how can we work together? A well-known Nigerian saying tells us to "wrap our minds together" and only God enables us to do that. In Galatians 5:13-15 (NIV), Paul tells the church "...do not use your freedom to indulge your sinful nature;

rather serve one another in love. The entire law is summed up in a single command: love your neighbor as yourself. If you keep on biting and devouring each other, watch out or you will be destroyed by each other." We must remember that we cannot all be first. Even twins in the womb are born one at a time. Every group can have only one leader, but God says that leader must be a servant to the others, or that leader will fail. Progress does not come without order and cooperation. Education is important, but only God gives us the spiritual weapons needed to overcome our enemies.

Jesus profoundly changed my life at age seven, but my education at Lancaster Bible College profoundly changed my worldview and equipped me with the tools I needed for the work God is giving me.

Human beings are made in the image of God. The image of God is reflected in the ability of the mind of humans to grasp godly concepts, such as understanding justice, beauty, honor, and compassion and how to distinguish between good and evil. The human brain is designed to learn these attributes through education. Education is not just formal training. It is also a very dynamic, complex process that begins with our families and our cultures. It continues through our friends, leaders, and everyone we encounter, including our enemies, as we have seen in my life story. Because the nature of humanity is fallen, we can use education as an instrument for good or for evil.

During the long and dangerous walk through the deserts and the bush of South Sudan, my people prayed and sought help from God. In those years of hardship and suffering as refugees, my people leaned on his everlasting arms. I was constantly in need of God's help to put all these things into proper perspective as I witnessed the loss of life and limb of those around me. In the refugee camp, the highlights of my life were participating in church through singing, praying, teaching, and fellowship. At the same time, I saw that constant danger, deprivation, and desperation robbed so many of hope. I saw that those without hope lost their initiative to make life better for themselves. In certain ways, we were all interdependent, but those who lost hope became so dependent that they seemed incapable of making decisions about important areas of their lives. I also observed that the life-saving help that came to us in Sudan was not simply from a group of people but a whole network of supportive services from various places. Help came from people of good will and compassion who worked under organizations that were publicly supported. Their support provided them with the prestige and political power needed to accomplish their purposes. I decided this would be the best way for me to work with my people, and this led to the formation of my Sudan Rebirth Ministry.

Nehemiah has long been my hero in the Bible, because his situation seems so similar to the situation of the "Lost Boys." Just as Nehemiah was exiled to Persia, I was exiled to America. Just as Nehemiah prayed for ways to restore hope to his people, I have been praying for ways to restore hope to my people in South Sudan. Just as the king of Persia offered Nehemiah resources to help him restore his people, America has supplied great sources of help for the "Lost Boys" to come to the U.S.A. Nehemiah's mission was to rebuild the walls of the city, which would give the people protection. He was a giver of hope, which would allow them to rebuild their lives. In a similar way, I want to provide hope for my people by educating those whose minds are being wasted through loss of opportunity, to restore faith through the study of God's word, and to bring healing through medical services and clean water.

The people of South Sudan formed a new nation because we were dissatisfied with the old. At the same time, many good characteristics existed within the old nation, which benefited the people and enabled them to flourish. One of our old sayings declares, "do not throw out the baby with the bathwater." It is the dirty water we want to discard, not the precious baby. In the same way, we want to preserve the things about the old system that contributed to the safety and welfare of the people. So, the work of those in the new nation is to discern exactly what will be in the best interests of the people.

27

My Vision

When I was a small boy, I had a vision. My brothers and cousins and I were staying in cattle camp, tending our families' livestock. One night I had a very vivid dream: I was standing before a large gathering of our people, wearing a white collar. In the morning, I shared my dream with my cousins. They laughed at me. "No one in our family has ever been a pastor. You cannot be a pastor." When I kept talking about my dream, they beat me.

Soon after, when our home area was attacked, our whole world was turned upside down. During the terrible times when we were running away from our homes, I didn't think much about what I would do in the future. I just wanted to stay alive. We ran hundreds of miles to what we thought was a safe place in Ethiopia. Many died on the way.

However, once I reached the crowded refugee camps, first in Ethiopia, then in Kenya, hope for a place in God's work began to come back. I learned to read so I could study the Bible, and I became a leader among the Sudanese people in the camp.

As you will remember, I was chosen along with other "Lost Boys" to come to America. I came to Houston on March 7, 2001, and the next morning some missionaries from First Baptist Church came to visit us. They saw the potential in me and they nominated me to be a leader of the Bible studies for the "Lost Boys" in my apartment. They also asked me to be the representative for the Sudanese communities in Houston, which is over 500 people. In Houston, we started the Sudanese Community Fellowship, and I was their pastor. While I was in Houston, I attended Houston Community College and took English classes. Then I transferred to the College of Biblical Studies.

Jacob and Rebecca with their children, Biar, Angeth and Ayiei

While I was visiting a friend in Lancaster, Pennsylvania in 2003, I met a First United Methodist pastor named Kent Kroehler. He encouraged me to transfer to Lancaster Bible College, from which I graduated in 2011. He has been so helpful to me, and recommended that I further my studies at Asbury Theological Seminary in Wilmore, Kentucky.

During this time, my vision began to take a more definite shape. I knew I wanted to help my people, but I was not certain how or where to start.

When I first returned to Sudan, my brother and cousins told me, "We want you to be a leader for our community in the government, not to be a pastor." They were very strong in their opposition to my calling. So, I went to my uncle, who is the most respected member of our family, and I explained my vision. He told the whole family, "To be a spiritual leader is more important than being a member of the government. Who are you to stand against the will of God? Let Jacob do his work!" As things have turned out, those relatives are now very supportive of my vision.

In 2008, I returned to South Sudan and part of my childhood dream became true—I received the white collar I had seen in my childhood dream. I was ordained in the Episcopal Church in Sudan, first as a deacon and then as a pastor.

All through the years of separation from my home and my relatives, I was eager for news of our people. Where is this one? Where is that one? What has become of our hometown? The news was not good. Many of my friends had been killed by invaders or died while running away. Our home district was devastated by the fighting which swept back and forth across Sudan. Nearly three million of our people were scattered into refugee camps in other countries.

I began to identify with one of the heroes of the Old Testament: Nehemiah. Like me, he was an exile, living and working in a foreign country. The news from his home city of Jerusalem broke his heart. The walls of the city were broken down and the people who lived there were not following God's ways. They were suffering and they had no protection. The ones who were in exile wanted to return, but it was not safe. Nehemiah was so upset he couldn't do his work properly. His employer, the King of Babylon, graciously allowed him to return to do what he could to restore Jerusalem, beginning with rebuilding the walls.

In 2014, I returned to Sudan and was overwhelmed with the needs I saw there. Just like Nehemiah, I knew something had to be done, so I started an organization. I asked some friends to join the board, and we found a lawyer here in Kentucky who knew how to set up a 501(c)(3) organization. But we needed a name. The vision that kept coming to me was the hope we had when we were running away from our home. We feared for our lives at night, but we had hope when the sun came up. We had another day to live. I thought about the millions of my own Sudanese people who have been driven from their homes, especially children, and their hope for a brighter future. So we named our mission Africa Sunrise Communities.

My passion and vision have led to the founding of the Africa Sunrise Communities ministry. The sunrise is the main source of African prosperity. We expect the sunrise to come, giving us the light we need for hunting, farming, and all other activities that are dependent upon the sun. The sunrise is the life and joy of Africa, because we wait for the morning to come so we can do our work. When the sun goes down, everything we have been doing stops because there is no light. Without the sunrise and the sunlight of the day, there is no life in Africa, and there is no hope for the future. The sunrise is the beginning of a new day, with new hopes and new opportunities. That is why I have chosen "Sunrise" as part of our name.

My organization's mission statement declares: "Africa Sunrise Communities is a faith-based, nonprofit organization with the mission of restoring communities, empowering refugees, and reconciling relationships in East Africa."

When I fled my home at the age of 7, friends escaped with me, among them Gabriel Kwai and Paul Deng. All three of us were eventually brought to the United States as "Lost Boys." Although ending up in different American communities, we have remained in touch and are all now involved in Africa Sunrise Communities.

Africa Sunrise Communities has some ready-made advantages over other organizations when it comes to providing help to the South Sudanese people. This organization is run by nationals who understand the cultural dynamics and sensitivities of the South Sudanese. We have the advantage of knowing the languages and culture of the South Sudanese, making it easier to gain acceptance in their hearts.

Only 20% of the people in South Sudan can read and write. The country has lost three generations to illiteracy, as a result of the long civil war between Muslims in the North and Christians in the South. Now, South Sudan is a country where 80% of the population is illiterate because the Muslim government of Sudan for 60 years denied them the opportunity to go to school. Without education, the South Sudanese have no hope of rebuilding their country.

Jacob and child

Jacob and refugees in Bweyale Camp, Uganda

The fact that the children have few opportunities for education is a tragedy not only for them but for South Sudan as a whole. Illiteracy impacts the prospects for their becoming leaders in their country. South Sudan cannot flourish as a nation if no one does anything to help provide the appropriate education for its youngest citizens. Education will help them rebuild our nation.

Although the nation of Sudan was split into two countries in 2008, the new country of South Sudan did not get away from serious problems. We were free from domination by the Muslim north, but we still had the ancient problem of tribal conflict. There are two main ethnic groups in South Sudan, Dinka and Nuer, and many smaller tribes. They cannot enjoy the peace that should have come with becoming a new nation, but they continue to fight and kill each other.

In August of 2012, I came to Asbury Theological Seminary in Wilmore, Kentucky. My main goal in seminary was to seek a Master of Arts degree in Intercultural Studies. This multidisciplinary program focuses on learning about other cultures and developing skills in negotiating across cultural boundaries. Cross-cultural conflicts are one of the biggest problems in Africa, due to the lack of understanding and misinformation between cultures. I see God's word as the only viable bridge that can cross those gaps, gain the respect of all the people, and enable them to work together for the good of all.

By God's grace, I graduated from Asbury Seminary in May of 2016 and finished my last classes in August of that year. Now I am seeking to fulfill the vision that God has given me to return to help my people in the new nation of South Sudan, as well as in the Sudanese churches. I have spent almost half of my life in America, but in my spirit, I am a citizen of both America and Sudan. I was born in Sudan and became a naturalized citizen in America so, in a sense, I feel like I am half African and half American.

When Nehemiah returned to Jerusalem, he did not know the extent of the people's problems. He did know, however, that they needed one thing: a wall. That seemed to be a good place to start to address all the other problems his people might have. His first act when he arrived in his hometown was to take a secret survey of the situation. He went around at night and made a list of everything that was broken. Then when he gave his assessment to the community, they all agreed they should build the wall.

In the same way, I am committed to conducting my own evaluation of what needs to be done to help my fellow South Sudanese come to enjoy the abundant life God has promised. At this time, I cannot claim to know all the needs of my people, but I am convinced that Africa Sunrise Communities can make a huge difference. Also, I am not certain which is the best place for me to start: in my home town of Bor, or the capital city of Juba, or in the refugee camps in Uganda, Kenya, and Ethiopia. However, I do know two things which must be done: provide education for children and proclaim the message of peace and reconciliation to the warring factions.

My vision is to start with a school. When I was a child in the refugee camp, I remember being so excited to have a piece of charcoal to write with and a piece of cardboard to write on so that I could learn the alphabet. I want to provide this same opportunity for others. I want to be like Nehemiah in the Old Testament.

Since our tribe had become Christian before our desperate march seeking safety in 1987, many of our men had Bibles and when we hid in the jungles during the day the older men would spend a lot of time reading to and discussing the Bible with us boys. My heart was touched by Nehemiah as he asked the Persian King, whom he was serving, if he could return to his country to help restore the city walls of Jerusalem which had been broken by their enemies.

The Dinka have a long history of having been the recipients of Christian outreach. Missionaries first came to Sudan in 1905. European missionaries over the years have come and attempted to spread the Gospel of Jesus Christ to the largely animist people who inhabit this region. Some have seen the truth of the resurrection. Most, however, have rejected the message of our Lord as being a European message with little application to the Dinka people. An early English missionary, after years of trying to bring the Dinka the Good News, on his deathbed described them as a "hard-headed" people who would not come to faith by an outsider. "Only one of their children will be able to convert them," he is reported as saying. Right now, only 5% of the Dinka identify themselves as Christian (1% are Muslim, the remaining 94% worship idols, animals, ancestors, or various aspects of the natural world). God has raised up one of their children, me, and has been uniquely preparing me for the ministry before me.

I see myself as a modern-day Nehemiah. My vision is that of a missionary ministry designed to reach the people of Southern Sudan whose lives have been shattered by many years of civil war. This ministry will restore hope to the Dinka people through an active application of faith in our Lord, access to biblical truth, and basic education. I believe strongly that I have been called, from the minute I was ordained as a deacon, to serve God in whatever capacity I am able to. Now as a priest, I have a greater role to play in giving God's service to God's people.

Nehemiah was a captive Israelite who had become a trusted servant to the King of Babylon. When Nehemiah received a report that his home city, Jerusalem, was in ruins, the king offered his support. Like Nehemiah, I am in exile in America. Many generous Americans have "bought into" my vision, first by supporting me through many years of study, and now by joining me through Africa Sunrise Communities. He has brought me this far, and I pray for strength and power as he continues working with me.

Even though I have been blessed by my time in the United States, I have never desired to permanently settle here. Even before I came to America I felt a calling to return to my country and restore hope to my people as well. As a young boy growing up in the refugee camp of Kakuma, I was active in our Anglican church and loved to lead the people in worship.

Even before Nehemiah went back to Jerusalem, he had to deal with a difficult decision: In the big task ahead of his people (rebuilding the walls), which resources the local people could provide, and which resources must come from outside. Jerusalem had plenty of good workers and some people with leadership skills, even though they were disorganized. They also had plenty of stones, although they were all knocked down. What they lacked was good timber, so Nehemiah asked the king for a letter to Asaph, keeper of the king's forests, to provide him with beams for the gates and other fixtures (Nehemiah 2:8 NIV). Even though the wars in South Sudan have destroyed many of the resources we need to rebuild our nation, we do have citizens who are good workers and some local materials. However, our people are very poor economically, so we must find some resources from outside.

For that reason, I must have two organizations. I must organize Africa Sunrise Communities in South Sudan as an NGO (non-governmental agency). This is the entity which will be granted permits to work within the country, hire employees, provide organizational support, and so forth. It will be the umbrella agency under which we will be allowed to establish schools, churches, medical clinics, pastor training programs, and whatever other programs we find to be necessary. The second organization is already in place and has the same name: Africa Sunrise Communities. However, this one is based in America and seeks to raise those resources which are not available in South Sudan at this time. Already a number of people have joined this effort because they believe in our vision for South Sudan. My prayer is for wisdom and discernment to know which needs can be met locally and which needs require help from abroad.

There is another part of Nehemiah's vision that I want to help our people accomplish, but it is totally impossible by human effort. Only God can make it happen. In his great prayer at the beginning of his mission (Nehemiah 1:5-11 NIV), Nehemiah confessed the sins of his people, the Israelites. He admitted that they had broken God's laws and suffered greatly because of their disobedience. The many tribes of South Sudan have suffered greatly, not only because of the oppression from the north, but because they have behaved badly toward each other. For many generations, we have lived in fear and poverty because we have not lived in peace as neighbors, as God commanded. The cycle of killing and stealing each other's cattle and fighting for control of the government must stop. We cannot make progress until those old tribal hatreds are put behind us. Many well-meaning people have tried to stop the violence, but it is impossible unless God intervenes. Only when we are broken before Him and commit to living by His commands can genuine peace come. That is my prayer.

Also, in his prayer, Nehemiah reminded God of the promise He had made:

"......If you are unfaithful, I will scatter you among the nations, but if you return to me and obey my commands, then even if your exiled people are at the farthest horizon, I will gather them from there and bring them to the place I have chosen as a dwelling for my name." (Nehemiah 1:8-9 NIV).

Our Sudanese people have been uprooted from their homes and scatted among many nations. While they may have found safety and relief in those refugee camps and in host nations, it is not home. As I often say, "Home is always home." So many of my people want to return to the place of their birth, the soil from which they were driven. I believe God will bring them back to help rebuild our country, but only on one condition: that we agree to "obey my (His) commands." Someone must tell them, like Nehemiah did, that God wants to restore them according to His justice, His mercy, and His promise.

It has taken years of prayer and seeking God's will for me to come this far along in my desire to be a Nehemiah figure for my people. Many times, I have recognized my human weakness in this task and in that frame of mind I have become discouraged about our people ever being able to go back to what they once had. Then I realized that God did not want us to go back to what was but to establish a new work and bring our people into a globalized society in our land! Now I understand better why this has to be God's work, because my human soul will always yearn for what we had because it cannot comprehend the future as God can. Just as Nehemiah had to redirect his people when they became discouraged because they were looking through their human eyes at the magnitude of the work and the hostility of their enemies, I will constantly have to seek God's views for my direction. God graciously reminds me that he will be the builder; I will simply be the worker.

This is the vision that God has given me: "to help the people of South Sudan lift the quality of life in our country: spiritually, educationally, economically, physically, and socially—by God's grace."

Jacob Guot

Made in the USA
Lexington, KY
12 May 2018